To Don Alber
From George Griffin 2003

HIGH PLAINS THUNDER

Supermodified Racing in the Midlands

BOB MAYS

Fastrack Publishing

HIGH PLAINS *THUNDER*

Supermodified Racing in the Midlands

© 2002 by Bob Mays

Published by:
Fastrack Publishing
4268 Knox St.
Lincoln, NE 68504-1954

First Printing: March 2002

Cover photograph by: Leroy Byers
Contents page photograph by: Jim Penney
Printed by: Walsworth Publishing Company

Printed and bound in the United States of America

ISBN 0-9710805-0-X

All rights reserved. Except for the quoting of brief passages for the pupose of review, no part of this book may be reproduced or stored in an electronic retrieval system, without prior written permission of Bob Mays or Fastrack Publishing.

This book is dedicated to,

Bud and Myrna Mays,

*two people who allowed a little boy to dream, and
encouraged him to seek out those dreams and make them come true.*

*It is also dedicated to all those that paid the
ultimate price to participate in the sport of automobile racing.*

Contents

Introduction..................6

Acknowledgements..................9

Evolving to Extinction: The Plains States Supermodified, 1955-1983..................12

Chapter 1
Kansas City Here We Are
Kansas City, Missouri, 1955-1972..................14

Chapter 2
The Jayhawkers
Topeka, Kansas, 1958-1972..................40

Chapter 3
Birthplace of the Nationals
Knoxville, Iowa, 1958-1972..................60

Chapter 4
Racin' on Tulsa Time
Tulsa, Oklahoma, 1960-61, 1966-1983..................84

Chapter 5
81 & Counting
Wichita, Kansas, 1962-1981..................106

Chapter 6
Husker Heros
Lincoln, Nebraska, 1964-1974..................124

Chapter 7
Small Town Thunder
Central Nebraska, 1967-1978..................144

Chapter 8
Hot Cars in the City
Oklahoma City, Oklahoma, 1967-1981..................164

Chapter 9
Marshall Dillon's Posse
The Merrick Circuit of Western Kansas, 1968-1978...184

Chapter 10
League of Champions
National Championship Racing Association, 1971-1981..................198

Epilogue..................216

Track Champions..................218

Index..................224

Capitol Beach Speedway in Lincoln, NE, has a full house and a full field. (Bill Smith collection)

Nebraska State Fair, same thing, full house, full field. (Bob Mays collection)

Introduction

When I was a kid growing up in Lincoln, Nebraska, my family's regular Sunday night ritual was going to the stock car races at Capitol Beach Speedway. My earliest memories in life, were of those old coupes and coaches flying around that little bull ring in West Lincoln. Like all the other kids that built little race tracks in the dirt between the wheel fence and the bleachers at the "Beach", I had my favorites. Men like Gordie Shuck, Buck Fallstead, John Wilkinson and all the others that climbed into those crates were bigger than life, and tougher than Superman, to a little kid that could still count all his birthdays on his fingers without using any of them twice.

Then on every Labor Day weekend we'd go see the Big Cars (a/k/a.) sprint cars) run at the Nebraska State Fair. The modifieds at Capitol Beach were wonderful fun because all my heroes drove them, but at the fair, the cars were the stars! They even had names for the most formidable of them. "Black Deuce," "Offy Killer," "Belle of Belleville" and "Circle Deuce" were the names of finely tuned, sleek machines that ran, not at some slam-bang Sunday night bull ring, no, these babies were the cream of the crop, the top of the heap, and they only came around once a year. I had heard of places like Indianapolis and Daytona, but those were far off places that only existed on movie screens and TV. My real life heroes were at the Beach and the fair.

One Sunday afternoon, my dad told me that there would be a special show at Capitol Beach that night. Now, up to that time a special show meant a 50 lap feature instead of the usual 25. "They're going to be running hoodoo wagons tonight," my dad said. HooDoo Wagons? What the heck were hoodoo wagons? Dad, reading the confusion on my face, said, "I think they are something like the big cars." WOW! What could be something like big cars and race at the Beach too! Needless to say, I was the first one in the car when supper was done and my dad couldn't drive to the races fast enough for me that evening. As we approached the entrance to Capitol Beach, up ahead was a truck towing a race car. I could tell right away that this was no ordinary coupe or coach, and it definitely was not a big car either. It had a sleek nose and hood, like a big car, but it also had a full roll cage and a short stubby tail that made this car a breed apart.

Standing in the ticket line that night was the first time I'd ever heard the word "supermodified." It came over the public address system loud and clear: "...THE SUPERMODIFIEDS ARE GETTING READY TO ROLL ONTO THE TRACK!" the announcer blared. I think I about tore my dad's arm out of its socket getting through the crowd that night. What I saw before me was more than I could comprehend. Big cars were generally the same shape, sleek and aerodynamic. The regular Beach cars were either a coupe or sedan of pre-war vintage. But these supermodifieds, each one was so different there just didn't seem to be words to describe them. While one would look only slightly smaller than a Sunday night stock car, another would look like a big car, only with a cage over the cockpit. Still another looked like a sprint from the front and a stock car from the back! To tell you the truth, I don't really remember much about the racing that night. What I remember is that each and every car that lined up was unique. I would find out later, a true supermodified is unique, and that's about the best way to describe them.

That night's events would be the only time supermodifieds ever ran at the Beach. After that I quit calling the competition at Capitol Beach "stock cars." From then on, they were "modifieds." It wasn't too long before the modifieds grew wings and fire breathing OHV motors. The seeds were sown for supermodifieds at the Beach.

Capitol Beach was razed after the 1962 racing season to make way for a housing development. The day I learned of the Beach's demise, I was sad, but Eagle Raceway and Midwest Speedway were built in 1963, so now there were twice as many chances to see my heroes. They were still in the coupes, but these coupes were the fastest around. The death of another friend was realized in 1964, as the coupes were out and real honest to goodness supermodifieds were in at Midwest and Eagle! This time there would be no sadness however, the modifieds had been good friends, but this was not as much a death, as it was a metamorphosis.

It was a wonderful year, as men like Lloyd Beckman, Rex Jordan, and Frank Brennfoerder were able to prove all over again what great racers they were and as star-struck young boy grew into an adult, so too did the supermodifieds grow into sprint cars. I didn't forget, however, those early days, the days of hoodoos and supers.

It has been 40 plus years since I saw that first supermodified at the front gate of Capitol Beach and I still struggle trying to describe them. I guess it will have to be enough to describe them as the most radical, wild, and sometimes, just plain goofy cars that have ever raced. In the old days of road racing, when a club wanted to hold a race with few or no rules, they called it a "Formula Libre" race, "Libre" being French for liberal (or something like that). In the old days of circle track racing, when we wanted to have a race with few or no rules, we called the thing a supermodified! These cars were different from any other class of racing (or, for that matter, each other) and they were called different names in various parts of the country. Monikers such as bugs, skeeters, sportsmen, semi-supermodifieds, coupsters, hoodoo wagons, super sports, caged sprints jet coupes and just plain modifieds were among the names that local tracks hung on the supermodifieds.

Just who first coined the word supermodified will probably never be known, but it started showing up in the early 1950's. The pre-war coupes and coaches, that came to be known as modified stock cars, were supplanting the midgets as the people's choice on the short tracks, and as the competition became keener among the modifieds, some free thinking racers figured out that the most valuable speed tool they had in their toolbox was the hacksaw. First the fender wells were enlarged, then cut off completely, frames and rear ends were narrowed, bodies were chopped and channeled. Some tracks came up with rules to keep the cars "stock" while other tracks embraced the changes that these hacksaw handling unencumbered theorists were making. By the early 1960's, what was left of the original pre-war body work was completely disregarded in favor of sheet metal which was cut and formed over the roll cage, engine and fuel tank. It wasn't long before the fiberglass sprint car noses, hoods, and tails made their way into the class. It was because of this constantly evolving process, in every region covered by this book, that supermodifieds became sprint cars. And so it was, that one track at a time, the supermodified era ended on the great plains.

Within the pages of this book, you will find jalopies of the 1950's and sprint cars of the 1980's. Somewhere in-between are supermodifieds. Ask 10 people to define supers and you'll get, if you're lucky, only nine different answers. Because there was no national sanctioning body for supers, with the exception of the National Championship Racing Association, rules have been whatever the local track or regional club made up. Therefore, supers are different things to different people. For that reason, this book is separated into chapters on each area, with each chapter title taking the name of the dominant track of the region. I'll try to show how, year by year, the super went from jalopy to sprint, (or dirt champ). Since not every track bent the rules at the same time, the time line will be different for each one. Knoxville, IA, for instance, saw its first super come through the gate in 1958. Oklahoma City, OK, didn't see one until 1967.

Defining the end of the supermodified era in each area is less precise. In the case of tracks such as Knoxville, Topeka, etc., where the caged sprints took over rather quickly, the early 1970's seem to be the most logical end of the line. Why is that, you say? Well, starting in 1971, all the sprint car sanctioning bodies in the country mandated cages as standard equipment. Most had allowed cages as optional until then. In 1969, in many instances, a roll cage was what separated a super from a sprint car. In 1970, the separation became fuzzy and, by 1971, it had disappeared altogether.

Of course there were still tracks that ran the 100-inch wheelbase cars in the Oklahoma/Kansas area. Those tracks seemed dedicated to keeping the supermodified as a distinct form of motorsports. But even with the NCRA keeping a tight lid on rules, it wasn't enough. After the 1981 season, NCRA changed the name of its premier division from supermodified to dirt champ. The metamorphosis was complete. How they changed and the men that changed them is what you will see within these pages.

But for now let's go back to 1958, or 1961, or 1967, or whenever supermodifieds first came through the pit gate at your favorite track, and let's get ready to see some of the wildest short track cars to ever cut mud ....

...AND NOW, LADIES AND GENTLEMEN, THE SUPERMODIFIEDS ARE GETTING READY TO ROLL ONTO THE TRACK!

World's first supermodified? Gordie Shuck readies himself for battle at a Hot Rod race in Beatrice, NE, during the summer of 1950. His car, which made its debut in 1948, was built out of a variety of parts. The frame came from a 1927 Studebaker; the hood and grill were from a 1932 Ford; the tail was originally a hood off a Studebaker Starlite Coupe; the cockpit sides were front fenders, turned upside down, off a brand new 1949 Ford police car that had been wrecked during its first week in service! (George Edeal photo)

Acknowledgments

Writing a book like this might seem easy at first glance, just get a bunch of pictures and write a bunch of captions, but finding pictures of stuff that happened 30, and in some cases 40 years ago can get to be an overwhelming job. Luckily for me, I've been able to find a few devoted individuals who care very much about the racing history of their region. It is because of them that this work exists.

The first guy I have to thank, the guy most responsible for the success of this project, is Mike Pogue of Claremore, OK. There are, no doubt, people in this country who have larger photo collections than Mike, but I don't know if anyone has a larger collection of supermodified photos than him. It is because of Mike that the Tulsa, Wichita, Merrick and NCRA chapters are as complete as they are. He acquired the photo and negative collections of Tulsa, OK, shooter, Tim Malone, and Wichita, KS, photographer, Jerry Leep, as well as digging up other old photos from here and there. Mike also came up with some Kansas City gems from the camera of Lou Ash. I had never met Mike before kicking this project into high gear in 1998, and now I count him as a very good friend. It has been a gas sitting in the Pogue living room for hours and hours agonizing over which shots to use in the book, as well as traveling all over Northeast Oklahoma listening to veteran racers tell their stories. Thanks, Mike.

Another big thank you has to go to Knoxville, IA's Bob Wilson. Bob was one of the first people I contacted, and his diligence in keeping Knoxville's history alive is one of the reasons that facility enjoys the reputation it does.

Two more Knoxville resident's that have had a big impact on this work, are Tom Schmeh and Craig Agan of the National Sprint Car Hall of Fame & Museum in Knoxville. Both these men have been instrumental in helping me get in contact with people that could help in this thing. If ever you have the chance to visit the Hall of Fame in Knoxville, do so. All the people associated with that facility, are among the friendliest in the business.

One more fellow who has helped me with contacts is, ol' Sunflower JR himself, Jim Richardson of Wichita. In addition to hooking me up with Mike Pogue, Jim steered me to long time Wichita photographer, Ken Greteman and the man that heads up the Kansas Antique Racers (KAR), Tom Barclay. Ken provided me with his remaining negative collection, while both Jim and Tom have been invaluable assets in identifying many of the images therein.

I doubt the Kansas City chapter of this book would have been possible without the help of veteran KC racer, Charlie Kraft. Charlie has been one of the most ardent supporters of this book, and has dug up many photos, and information on Kansas City racing. Veteran KC photographer, and long-time friend, Ken Simon, dug into his archives for several great shots. Two other men that have helped with Kansas City information are Luther Brewer and Jim Penney. Brewer, the racing postmaster, from Drexel, MO, provided numerous tidbits about both the KC and Topeka area. Penney set me gobs of newspaper and magazine articles on the racing in and around Kansas City. Junior Parkinson and his dad, Ralph Sr., helped me contact many of the Kansas City racing veterans that are highlighted in these pages as well. One of those, Bud Hunnicutt pitched in some great shots of the early racing at Olympic and Riverside, for which I am truly grateful. I certainly cannot forget Jon Backlund, who chipped in with some great stuff and was a great host while I searched out the KC area for super information.

Oklahoma City would have been impossible to cover had it not been for Shane Carson. The son of long time OKC promoter, Bud Carson, as well as being one of the best sprint car racers in the world the last 20 years and a promoter himself, Shane let me sit in his garage poring over boxes and boxes of old Mar-Car photos, after one of his World of Outlaws promotions was rained out on a Sunday afternoon in the spring of 1999. It's easy to see that Shane very proud of his father's legacy in Oklahoma City.

Another 1999 rainout provided me with the opportunity to meet Topeka, KS racing photographer, Tom Powell. When the first night of a two night WoO was canceled at Heartland Park, I ended up in Tom's garage looking through boxes of racing negatives that Tom and his father had shot from 1958 through the early 1970's at the Mid-America Fairgrounds and Shawnee Speedway.

A guy that helped immensely with the Topeka and Kansas City chapters, was Rich Still of Bahama, NC. Rich is the son of long time Topeka car owner, Roy Still, and has spent the last few years researching his dad's career. The result is several large volumes of race clippings out of newspapers, both racing and dailies, all over the Midwest.

On several occasions I've been the guest of Beryl Ward in her lovely Concordia, KS, home to research this book along with other projects. Beryl and her late husband, Les, were corespondents for National Speed Sport News, covering most of the Midwest. Beryl's vivid memory of over 60 years of Belleville, KS, racing history, along with Les' extensive photo collection which Beryl diligently maintains, helped a great deal in filling out many details of the Topeka chapter.

Good buddy, Dean Ward, was able to dig up quite a few of the late George Edeal's photos for the Central Nebraska chapter, and old friend, Jerry Jacobs chipped in with some to fill out the last few years of that chapter.

For helping with the Lincoln, NE. chapter, I first have to give a big thank you to Joe Orth. Joe's photography has been a fixture in the Lincoln racing community for many years, and he continues to do an excellent job. Glenna Barnett loaned me some of her late husband, Gene's, negatives which filled in much of the early years of Lincoln Supermodified racing. I couldn't leave the Lincoln chapter without a big thank you to my buddies at the Nebraska Auto Racing Hall of Fame, especially Tony Glenn, Bo Nickolite, Bill Smith and Ray Valasek, for all their help.

Denver's favorite son, Leroy Byers, pitched in some of his brilliant photography to round out both the Lincoln and Knoxville chapters. Leroy's great shot of Harold Leep and Gene Gennetten at Amarillo in 1968 is still my all-time favorite racing photo and serves as the cover shot for this book.

I also need to thank Ruby Hill, whose husband, Bill, is an award winning author and historian, for proofing all these pages. Her first hand knowledge of the racers contained herein proved quite valuable, in addition to making sure all the X's and O's were in the right places.

Other people and organizations that provided valuable information were:

Lee Ackerman
Dave Argabright
Butch Bahr
Keith Barker
Lloyd Beckman
Jerry Bell
Duane Bender
Ralph Blackett
Bob Blazek
Ed Bowes
Frank Brennfoerder
Woody Brinkman
Allan Brown
Gerald Bruggeman
Roy Bryant
Bob Burdick
Mike Butcher
Buddy Cagle
Bruce Craig
Wayne Dake

Larry Dewell
Jerry Everhart
Ralph Forbes
Scott Fernyhough
Jim Gessford
Jim Goettsche
Lynn Grabill
Doug Haack
Stan Haack
Emmett Hahn
Dennis Hegel
Tim Hiatt
High Banks Hall of Fame & National Midget Auto Racing Museum
Bill Hill
Charles Hoffman
Jerry Holmes
Jefferson County (KS) Historical Society
Armin Krueger
Bob Lawrence
Harold Leep
Harold Lloyd Leep
Lincoln Journal & Star
Don McChesney
Bobby Moore
"Big Al" Murie
Nebraska State Historical Society

Denny Oltman
Larry Patterson
Dale Reed
Jim Riggins
Joe Saldana
Gordie Shuck
Dick Stelzer
Benny Taylor
Bob Trostle
Warren Vincent
Grady Wade
Ed Watson
Rick Watson
Monte Wellendorf
Ron Williams
Kyle Willingham
Randy Willingham
Jay & Pat Woodside
Ray Woodward

Heroes - All of my heroes have been race car drivers. To meet your first hero up close is as defining a moment in your life as anything that will ever happen to you. We don't know who the young fellow in this picture is, but his hero is, and has always been, Bud Hunnicutt, who stands beside him at Riverside Stadium in North Kansas City in 1962. (Bud Hunnicut collection)

11

Evolving to Extinction: *THE PLAINS STATES SUPERMODIFIED, 1955-1983*

1. The Jalopy. Stock cars, stock motors, stock everything. The Ford Flathead engine was the staple of the short tracks in the 1950's. Then along came the small block Chevy. Here, Larry Stromer is digging dirt. (George Edeal photo)

2. The Modified. Stock body, stock chassis, slightly modified overhead valve engine, and the biggest right front tire that money can buy. Don Schoenfeld is at the controls. Note, the building in the background is the Tulsa Expo Building where the Chili Bowl is held each year. (Mike Pogue collection)

3. The Bug. In this case, a cut down '34 Ford 4-door sedan real steel body, altered Model A frame, Corvette engine. The wheelman is Stan Haack. (George Edeal photo)

4. The HooDoo Wagon. Flat aluminum sheets cut to fit, make up the body. Chassis is a custom race unit from Culbert Automotive Engineering (CAE). Russ Brahmer steers. (George Edeal photo)

5. The Edmunds. The most popular body style in supermodified history is the one designed by Don Edmunds. Small, light and good looking, many builders put their cars inside Don's fiberglass. This one is chauffeured by Len Sherrell. (Mike Pogue collection)

6. The 100-Inch Car. Bud Carson hit on the original idea. When NCRA (which Carson helped create) came into existence in 1971, uniform rules resulted in a supermod for the 1970's. 100" wheelbase, self-starting, carburated and 305 cubic inch engine. This time it's Ray Crawford going for a spin. (Tim Malone photo)

7. The Sprint Car. Sprint cars needed cages. Supers had them. When most sprint clubs started allowing full coverage chrome moly life insurance for their drivers, the line between supermodified and sprint car blurred, then quickly disappeared, as tracks began offering weekly sprint shows with the same cars that had been running the supermodified class. Here, Eddie Leavitt has just won a big supermodified(?) race. (Beetle Bailey photo)

8. The Dirt Champ Car. In 1981 NCRA had a problem, all their cars were beginning to look the same. Solution: Plagiarize USAC's name for its premier class! They upped the cubic inches to 360 and legalized fuel injection also. Only Tulsa Speedway complained, but after a couple of years, they capitulated and the plains states supers had gone the way of the buffalo. Here we have Ernest Jennings. (Bob Mays photo)

Eddie Leavitt (Taylor Weld 94) pinches against the inside rail, as he tries to gain a spot at Jim Leighty's (22) expense. Taylor Weld, known to most racers as "Pappy," built this car in 1965 and crusaded it for many years in the Kansas City area, and all over the Midwest, with great success. The action depicted here happened at the Missouri State Fairgrounds in Sedalia in 1969. (Ken Simon photo)

Chapter 1
KANSAS CITY HERE WE ARE
KANSAS CITY, MISSOURI 1955-72

It was once said that if a car owner wanted a stand-on-the-gas driver, all he need do is pick a name out of the Kansas City phone book. It was, without a doubt, the toughest circuit in the country during the 1960's.

Three tracks operated in the metro-Kansas City area, Olympic Stadium in Kansas City, Missouri, Lakeside Speedway in Kansas City, Kansas and Riverside Stadium in Riversdie (North Kansas City,) Missouri. Olympic was the smallest (just under a 1/4 mile) but the most successful. Riverside was also a 1/4 mile and was quite successful, too. Lakeside was a big 1/2 mile, but suffered from a lack of consistent promotion. Together, these tracks produced some of the best drivers in the country throughout the 1950's and 1960's.

Central Missouri tracks such as Capital Speedway in Holts Summit and Sportsman Speedway in Marshall also developed some tremendous competition. Each year the KC and Central Missouri racers would get together for the Missouri State Championship race in Sedalia during the state fair. For many years this was one of the most prestigious races in the Show Me State. No one was fatally injured racing supers in the Kansas City area, although Ken Taylor was killed in 1966 at Marshall.

Kansas City 1955-56

"Wild Bill" Chennault drove Otto Haggart's clean coupe to the championship at Olympic Stadium in 1955. (Jim Penney collection)

Cab Forward - When Jerry Weld showed up at Riverside Stadium in 1955, everyone else went shopping for hack saws. Weld's "Flying Suitcase" was the first cut down car to appear in the Midwest and it caused a sensation. Jerry was the top rookie of 1955, then creamed the competition in '56 with 11 feature wins and the Riverside point title. (Jim Penney collection)

Bud Hunnicutt with his first ride at Riverside in 1956. Note the body on Bud's car has been moved forward for better weight distribution. Bud and Jerry Weld were good friends and the Flying Suitcase had a big effect on how this car was built. (Jim Penney collection)

Bud Wallis annexed five wins and finished second to Jerry Weld at Riverside in 1956. (Jim Penney collection)

Joe Walter, a top midget racer in the KC area, showed up a few times in the Carl's Hollywood Muffler Shop Special. (Jim Penney collection)

Eye of the Beholder? - Iron Head Cox is at the wheel of what has to be one of the ugliest cars ever built. There was no report of the car's accomplishments, but the fact that Ol' Iron Head is still around, after racing this thing, is an accomplishment in itself. (Jim Penney collection)

Many KC racers would run a flathead, as were the rules, for Riverside on Saturday night, then install an overhead valve motor for Sunday's open show at Olympic. Charlie Kraft could run with equal success at either place. (Jim Penney collection)

Kansas City 1957

The Power of Junior Hower - Perhaps the first true superstar of supermodified racing was Junior Hower. He was a veteran of the roadster wars in the 1940's and 1950's and when the supers came around Junior was leading the way. Here he is, celebrating another win at Riverside Stadium. Junior won most of the point titles that were handed out in the KC area in the 1950's. (Lou Ash photo)

Charlie Kraft finished sixth in points at Riverside Stadium, behind, Jerry Weld, Cliff Lilly, Red Snedeger, Bud Hunnicutt and Cecil Davis. (Charlie Kraft collection)

Jud McFarland (2) plows into a parked car at Olympic. (Lou Ash photo)

Kansas City 1958

Bud Hunnicutt carries the flag in his Bob Burns flathead after another convincing victory at Riverside Stadium. Hunnicutt won ten times in 1958 at the North Kansas City oval. This car was the first tube frame super in the Kansas City area, and while Burns was building it, he received plenty of advice about the folly of building a car out of "pipe." As the car won, Burns found himself giving out more advice than he was receiving. (Bud Hunnicutt collection)

Junior Hower gets the gold after another hard fought victory. Hower won nine main events at Olympic in 1958, three of them were 50 lappers, plus the big 100-lap season finale, to easily take the championship. (Lou Ash photo)

Kansas City 1959

Bud Hunnicutt (Burns 70) dices with teammate for the night, Dale McDaniels (Burns 15), as they enter the homestretch at Riverside. Hunnicutt won five times in 1959 at the North Kansas City oval, and notched his second straight title. (Lou Ash photo)

Tom DeVolder was another roadster veteran in the mold of Junior Hower. He came back from a three year layoff, after a passenger car accident, to post a win at Riverside in Ruth Bryson's 85. (Lou Ash photo)

Fins were all the rage in '59, and Jerry Weld thought they looked quite nice on his super. Jerry authored six wins at Riverside. (Lou Ash photo)

Dale McDaniels (18) chases Ken Harper (79) at Sedalia. McDaniels was the only serious threat to Junior Hower at Olympic in 1959, winning four mains and finishing second in points. (Lou Ash photo)

Kansas City 1960

Junior Hower (24) skirts around Ken Taylor (49) as he chases down Walter Sorrells (D-7) for the Missouri state title at Sedalia. (Lou Ash photo)

Virgil Chapman (27) ekes out a lead against Bud Hunnicutt (Burns 70) at Olympic. Chapman won Riverside titles in 1960 and '61. (Lou Ash photo)

Bob Williams was just getting his racing career started, but he already knew how to snarl at the camera. (Tom Powell photo)

Kansas City 1961

Weld, Inc. - The Weld family was very tight knit, and very competitive. Pappy Weld raised his sons to be free thinkers, as this shot from Olympic Stadium shows. Taylor's car (94) sits here beside Jerry's (93) and Greg's (92). Pappy had Bob Williams piloting his creation on this day while Jerry and Greg drove their own. (Lou Ash photo)

J. L. Cooper was a Kansas City fixture for many years. As you can see by this photo, even though Olympic was the smallest track in the region for supers, it didn't lack for seating. (Lou Ash photo)

Charlie Kraft and his "Black Magic" super get ready for Olympic action. (Lou Ash photo)

Gordon Woolley prepares for action in Jerry Gilbert's T at Olympic. (Lou Ash photo)

Kansas City 1962

Greg Weld came out with the first of his radical roadsters in 1962. He immediately became a force with which to be reckoned. (Bob Wilson collection)

The Missouri Charger - The legendary Al Murie is a character if ever there was one. He could race too, as many a KC competitor found out. Al's dad, Tom Murie was a racer in the 1920's and 1930's. (Al Murie collection)

Charlie Kraft (35) powers around another would-be contender at the Missouri State Championships in Sedalia. (Lou Ash photo)

Wes Ferrand had several good runs in Duane Vobach's crate. (Bob Wilson collection)

Kansas City 1963

Doug Rothgeb (16) leads a hungry pack at Riverside. Others that are identifiable are Al Baldus (37), Bud Hunnicutt (Bill Underwood 15) and Dick Sutcliffe (Jack Gibson 55). (Bud Hunnicutt collection)

The legendary Jud Larson sucks on a rag at speed in the Jerry Gilbert 19. When Larson decided to make his comeback, after a heart attack in 1959 took him out of racing, he jumped in Gilbert's supermodified. He annexed several feature wins, including a 75 lapper at Olympic on August 11, 1963. (Lou Ash photo)

Kansas City 1964

Olympic Stadium Champ for 1964, Ray Lee Goodwin, sits in the Duck Corum & Tom Purvis 13. Goodwin bought the car in 1965 and won the Olympic title again. (Tom Powell photo)

Jim McMurray was an ardent supporter of racing in the Kansas City area. After 23 years as a driver, Jim became an official, serving at Lakeside, I-70 and several other tracks. Here he is getting his sedan ready for another Olympic hoe-down. (Bob Morgan photo)

Ken Harper cuts a fast lap at Marshall in his home-made super. Harper's crate may not have been a show stopper, but it was fast. (Ken Simon photo)

Jay Woodside was still trying to shake off the effects of his 1962 crash at Topeka, when he climbed into this crate on an Olympic race night. (Leroy Byers photo)

1964 was Greg Weld's last year in supermodifieds before moving on to USAC. Here he is at Lakeside with his Speedway Motors sponsored mount. (Tom Powell photo)

Jon Backlund (top) and Stan Borofsky (bottom) pile up in front of Al Manning, Ken Williams (Bill Rhine 85) and Ray Lee Goodwin (13) in Olympic Stadium's turn four. (Bob Morgan photo)

Doug Burns (99), Jon Backlund (Charlie Kraft 4) and Kenny Weld (Weld 94) battle through Olympic's second corner. (Bob Morgan photo)

Ken Williams piloted Bill Rhine's highly modified '57 Chevy to several wins at Olympic. (Tom Powell photo)

Kansas City 1965

Jon Backlund ran some races in Charlie Stepps' 426 Plymouth big block. Handling problems were finally diagnosed when Backlund realized that, under acceleration, the front wheels were rarely touching the ground! (Tom Powell photo)

Kansas City 1966

Ray Lee Goodwin accepts the trophy at Marshall, MO, during the running of the Ken Taylor Memorial race in 1966. Goodwin and his Luther Brewer coupe were the scourge of Missouri and Kansas tracks in '66, winning titles at Olympic and the Mid-America Fairgrounds in Topeka. (Luther Brewer collection)

Cliff Lilly had this neat little Edmunds coupe for the Sunday night action at Olympic. (Bob Morgan photo)

Jerry Weld (93) flies into turn one ahead of Jon Backlund (Don Williams & Richard Foley 15). Backlund recorded his first of many wins at Olympic on this night. (Bob Morgan photo)

Luther Brewer plays flagman while his daughter, Brenda, plays trophy queen for Bob Williams at Olympic. Pappy Weld's super is the backdrop. (Luther Brewer collection)

Ed Leavitt leads Dale Moore (Bill Curtis 102) and Ken Baker (61) into turn one at Olympic. (National Sprint Car Hall of Fame collection)

Bob Willaims (Dick Howard 2) power slides in tandem with Ray Lee Goodwin (Brewer 97) at Olympic. (Luther Brewer collection)

Al Burke was another of the Olympic regulars that made this tiny oval one of the hardest places in the country at which to win. (Bob Morgan photo)

Kansas City 1967

Ed Fitzgerald (92) had a big year at Riverside Stadium in 1967, but during the Missouri State Modified Championship at Sedalia, he found himself in a less than advantageous position. Barney Bauerfind (2) is also figuring on a less than stellar pay day. (Ken Simon photo)

Fred Holman (XX) pushes across the bottom and Don Cooper (11) hangs on top, while Roy Carey (44) just tries to maintain in the middle. The action is at Sedalia. (Ken Simon photo)

Bob Ford (2) has Russ Hibbard (Sparky Carver 87) on his right rear as they exit Marshall's second bend. (Ken Simon photo)

Bob Williams and Pappy Weld had several stints together and, in 1967, they made it very tough on the competition at Olympic and elsewhere. (Leroy Byers photo)

Kansas City 1968

Gene Gennetten piloted Bill Rhine's Batmobile to Olympic point championships in 1967 and 1968. (Leroy Byers photo)

Ralph Parkinson and his crew look pleased with how his Edmunds kit-car turned out. The crewman on the left is a future sprint car racer of note, Ralph's son, Ralph Parkinson Jr., better known as Junior Parkinson. (Leroy Byers photo)

The first two rows of the 1968 Missouri State Championship race, at Sedalia, come around for the green flag. Russ Hibbard (Carver 87) and Dale Moore (Don Furr 96) make up the first row while Gene Gennetten (Rhine 300) and Jay Woodside (Weld 94) fill the second. Russ's brother Roy Hibbard won the annual affair. (Lewis Studio photo)

Tom Corbin (Keith Barker 43) digs in on the inside rail, while Russ Hibbard (Carver 87) gives the outside a go at the Missouri State Fairgrounds track in Sedalia. Both of these gentlemen were Central Missouri winners in 1968. (Ken Simon photo)

Gary Scott's "Wee 3" takes to the real high side in an effort to stay in front of Roy Hibbard (Miller Chevy 26) at Sedalia during the Missouri State Championships. Scott was a really nice guy who would die at Knoxville in 1982 in a horrible crash on the frontstretch. Because of that wreck, wings have been standard equipment at the Central Iowa oval since. (Ken Simon photo)

Kansas City 1969

Bob Williams piloted the Jack Cunningham Chevy to his first Olympic Stadium Championship in 1969. His domination was complete, with seven feature wins at the Kansas City oval, to go along with point titles at Knoxville and Topeka just for good measure. It may have been the best season ever by a Midwestern driver. (Tom Powell photo)

The Kelley Pontiac Special (which is Chevy powered) has a slight lead on Marvin Gibson in the Paul Sparks 62. Gibson came on strong on the Central Missouri scene in '69. (Ken Simon photo)

I-70 Speedway just outside of Odessa, MO, opened in 1969 and the KC race fans were treated to asphalt racing for the first time. Here, Jon Backlund, in the Charlie Aldrich roadster, battles with Joe Saldana (65). Backlund won the point championship of the inaugural season and established himself as a master of both dirt and macadam. (Jon Backlund collection)

Jay Woodside looks snappy as he tests the seat in the Keith Barker Chevy. Woodside was another that was equally adept on dirt or asphalt and proved it by winning the very first hard surface race in the KC area when I-70 Speedway opened in 1969. (Keith Barker collection)

Bob Williams (Cunningham 14) and Jay Woodside (Barker 3) contest a position, with Jon Backlund (Weld 94) lurking right behind in Olympic action. Backlund had knocked himself out of action the year before by hitting his head on the cage of Pappy Weld's car, so Weld curved the bars going from the front hoop to the rear hoop of the cage so Jon's noggin would have some clearance. (Bob Morgan photo)

The Arkansas Traveler - Bobby Ward (Mee2) came up from Conway, AR, and stole a bundle of money from the Missouri racers. Here he is putting Roy Hibbard (Miller 26) down a spot at the 1969 Short Track Championship at Sportsman Speedway in Marshall. (Ken Simon photo)

35

Ray Lee Goodwin (Brewer 97) looks over to Russ Hibbard (Carver 87) and seems to be thinking, "This job is tough enough without you passing me, too!" For his part, Hibbard looks like he is hoping the trophy girl is pretty. The track is Sedalia. (Ken Simon photo)

John Dix (144) gets to see how tight the competition really is at Olympic, as Ed McVay (Bill Roberts 47) J. L. Cooper (75) and a couple of other competitors scramble for open track. (Ken Simon photo)

Capital Speedway in Holts Summit, MO, is looking fast, as Jay Woodside (Barker 3) and Roy Hibbard (Miller 26) lock up. (Ken Simon photo)

The wings on these cars may not look like much by today's standards, but they seemed like good ideas at the time. Bob Williams (Cunningham 14) fights his on the low side, while Chuck Lynch (29) seems oddly in control under his double-element marvel. They're working Capital Speedway's clay. (Ken Simon photo)

Kansas City 1970

Gene Gennetten (Rhine 85) and Bob Williams (Gary Hanna 14) battle at Eagle Raceway in Nebraska. Gennetten's car in this photo is actually the former Batmobile number 300, with a sprint tail added, while Williams' ride is his 1969 triple championship car that Jack Cunningham sold to Gary Hanna in the off season. Gene Gennetten won his third Olympic point title in 1970. (Leroy Byers photo)

Ed Leavitt jumped into Keith Barker's powerful Don Brown built job in 1970 and collected firsts at Olympic, Marshall and the Missouri State Championship at Sedalia. (Ken Simon photo)

Comin' atcha' - Dick Sutcliffe brings his R & H Farms Chevy down I-70's pit road after a hot lap on the high banked half-mile asphalt. Note that Dick is running very little stagger on the rear, but has a bunch across the front. This angle also shows why Sutcliffe needs a good helmet, because his roll cage is only going to protect him from the eye brows down. (Ken Simon photo)

Jay Woodside (Hank Smith 5) and Roy Hibbard (Miller 26) fly through turn one at I-70. Unfortunately, poor attendance doomed the macadam plant's supermodified division, with stock cars taking over the 1/2 mile oval by midseason. (Ken Simon photo)

Whitey Harmon looks confident with his ex-Joe Booth machine. (Leroy Byers photo)

Kansas City 1971-72

Dismissing the notion that green is bad luck, Gene Gennetten piloted his emerald and sterling beauty to two more Olympic point crowns in 1971 and '72. (Bob Wilson collection)

Ed Leavitt (Barker 3) provided Gennetten with stiff competition all season, and won the 1971 Short Track Championship race at Olympic Stadium on August 8th. (Leroy Byers photo)

This Olympic Stadium traffic jam includes, Rick Murie, out front, with Gene Gennetten (3), J. L. Cooper (Long Chevy 32) and Jon Backlund (71) on the flanks. (Ken Simon photo)

Bill White (72) scoots around a lumbering sedan in Shawnee Speedway's first turn. This action took place at the little East Topeka track in 1959. (Tom Powell photo)

Chapter 2
THE JAYHAWKERS
TOPEKA, KANSAS 1958-72

Shawnee Speedway is where the Topeka supermodifieds were born, but it was at the Mid-America Fairgrounds where they came of age. Shawnee was a small operation throughout Topeka's supermod era, but a great many drivers learned their craft there. When the fairgrounds started weekly racing in 1961, Topeka immediately became a hot bed for the supers. In fact, the Jayhawk Nationals rivaled the Knoxville Nationals in the early years.

Ken Kneisler was Mid-America's first promoter, followed two years later by Bill Harrison. Kneisler formed the Mid-America Racing Association (MARA), and Harrison followed with the Jayhawk Racing Association (JRA). After Harrison, Jerry Weld took over the operation and ran it until his untimely death in 1970. Former car owner, Luther Brewer, then took charge.

Because of Mid-America's success, Shawnee soon gave up on the supers, and started a jalopy class which became something of a feeder system for the supermodifieds. Other area tracks to run special events for the supers were Belleville, Atchison and Emporia, Kansas. Chet Hamby (1961), Ken Williams (1969) and Jack Belk (1971) crashed to their deaths at the Mid-America Fairgrounds in supermodifieds.

Don Irwin had this beautifully done pickup bodied racer. Don took down three feature flags during the season. (Tom Powell photo)

Topeka 1958

Jerry Hayes was one of the top guns at Shawnee, winning five times, with this Larry Logan T. Jerry also won five in a row at Atchison Speedway. (Tom Powell photo)

Leon Spain assigned himself rookie status with this well built coupe. (Tom Powell photo)

41

Topeka 1959

It's pretty obvious that Bill Corwin knew his way around victory lane at Shawnee Speedway. He won five features at Shawnee in '59. (Tom Powell photo)

Buddy Marsh seems happy about his new ride, but the front end damage makes us wonder how far he'll get with it. (Tom Powell photo)

Bill Corwin (Jack Corwin IV) hasn't lost his touch with the ladies, and he can handle the flags too! (Tom Powell photo)

Topeka 1960

The Shawnee Speedway pickup/supermodified, circa 1960. (Tom Powell photo)

Bill Anno nabbed a dash victory. (Tom Powell photo)

Bill Cohee has all the necessary safety equipment in place to go pickup truck racing. NASCAR may have thought they invented truck racing but, as you can see from the last few pages, the Topeka boys had 'em beat by 35+ years! (Tom Powell photo)

Lyle Wittaker brought this piece to Shawnee, and ran pretty well! (Tom Powell photo)

43

Topeka 1961

Bill Corwin (Corwin 4) was the picture of consistency in 1961, grabbing the first championship ring that the Mid-America Fairgrounds handed out. (Tom Powell photo)

Harvey Shane must have ridden tall in the saddle; note that the cage on his car has been extended. (Tom Powell photo)

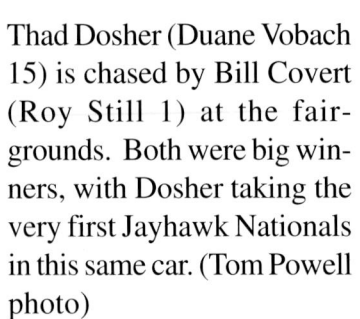

Thad Dosher (Duane Vobach 15) is chased by Bill Covert (Roy Still 1) at the fairgrounds. Both were big winners, with Dosher taking the very first Jayhawk Nationals in this same car. (Tom Powell photo)

Even though Gordon Woolley (Jerry Gilbert 19) didn't win any features in 1961 at Topeka, he was a real crowd pleaser. (Tom Powell photo)

Topeka 1962

Don Elliott won four features down the stretch to claim the '62 championship over Jack Belk. This would be the first of three straight Topeka titles for the Don Elliott/Roy Still combo. Here they are at Belleville in August of 1962. (L. A. Ward photo)

Bill Anno had a big problem at Belleville when the fence got in his way. The fence moved, in several directions at once, then Anno headed for the parking lot. He was not seriously injured. (Republic County Historical Society collection)

Claude Jefferies brought his "Little Jewell" out of retirement to run at Shawnee when they were suffering a car shortage. It was to no avail however, as promoter, Claude Berry, dropped the supers by seasons end. (Tom Powell photo)

Jerry Hayes came back from severe injuries in a 1960 sprint car crash to post some good finishes in Gary Hanna's "Golden Commando." (Bob Wilson collection)

46

Topeka 1963

Possibly the most underrated driver to race supermodifeds Jack Belk. Here he is, with his Al Weiland super, after winning the feature race on the last day of the 1963 North Central Kansas Free Fair at Belleville. Jack was killed at Topeka in 1971. (L. A. Ward photo)

Don Elliott (Still 1) streaks away from the trophy dash field at Belleville. Chasing Elliott are Bob Burdick (Rod Kettleson 3), Jack Belk (Weiland 37) and Art Dishinger. Belk won the dash and every thing else on this day. (L. A. Ward photo)

Red Andrews had Bud Wyatt's 111 humming, with several good runs. (Tom Powell photo)

Jeff (Smokey) Rice stands with his dad's super. The Rice's were solid fixtures throughout Topeka's supermodified history. They were one of the country's few full blooded Cherokee Indian racing teams. (Tom Powell photo)

Topeka 1964

Hittin' the Bricks - The story of the 1964 season at the Mid-America Fairgrounds was a simple one - crashes. In this one, Ray Lee Goodwin (Bill Cohee 12) runs away from the flying cement blocks as Wes Ferrand goes through the wall upside-down on top of Bob Williams. Art Dishinger (Charlie Stepps 28) watches closely, as he backs into the action. The only injuries were to the wall. (Tom Powell photo)

The cement wall that surrounded the fairgrounds track made for a distinctive trademark, but as a safety barrier it left much to be desired. Here, Dick Sutcliffe (Junior Hower 23) enlarges a hole made in an earlier wreck. Sonny King (131) hopes there are no cement blocks with his name on them. (Tom Powell photo)

Dick Sutcliffe (Hower 23) jumps the rail and heads for the wall again, while Ray Lee Goodwin (Duck Corum & Tom Purvis 13) slides to the inside. (Tom Powell photo)

Ray Lee Goodwin (Cohee 12) motordromes off the wall while Bob Williams (Gary Hanna 44) takes a more conservative approach. (Tom Powell photo)

Thad Dosher (Wyatt 111) doesn't look too happy about all the crashing going on. (Tom Powell photo)

49

Topeka 1965

"Hollywood" Ken Williams and his car owner, Roy Still, look satisfied with their fast Plymouth powered racer. Williams won the 1965 Topeka track title. (Tom Powell photo)

Jerry Weld was the happy winner of the Jayhawk Nationals after Wes Ferrand ran out of fuel on the last lap! (Tom Powell photo)

Californian, Dick Fries came east and won a feature at Topeka aboard the Wayne Wright 20. (Tom Powell photo)

Jack Belk skies the Luther Brewer 97 in turn two at the Mid-America Fairgrounds. Belk walked away after five or six cartwheels; the car went home in a basket. (Tom Powell photo)

Gordon Woolley (Ron Rosenburg 007) gets ready to bail out after a coming together with Bob Burns (70). Burns' car was designed like a slingshot dragster, with it's rear axle passing underneath the driver's knees! The car had great straight line speed, but was a nightmare in the corners. (Tom Powell photo)

Topeka 1966

Ray Lee Goodwin celebrates a Topeka dash win. Goodwin combined a fast car (Brewer 97) with consistent finishes to be Topeka's top point man in '66. (Luther Brewer collection)

Roger Christensen is ready for the '66 season to get going. Car owner, Jerry Hayes (third from left), looks happy with his new creation. (Tom Powell photo)

Shaken, Not Stirred - That's right, the name is Bond - James Bond, only this one is from Edwardsville, Kansas, and that's no Aston Martin. (Bob Morgan photo)

Buddy Marsh (George Clark 171) became the first winner of a night race at the Belleville High Banks, when Bill Harrison brought the Jayhawk Racing Association there in 1966. (Tom Powell photo)

Dick Sutcliffe was Ray Lee Goodwin's toughest competitor at Topeka, and everywhere else in the Midwest for that matter, in '66. Sutcliffe's car was one of the lightest supers ever built, thus it's owner/builder, Gary Hanna, dubbed it "the feather." (Ken Greteman photo)

Topeka 1967

Ray Lee Goodwin (Brewer 97) won his second straight Topeka crown in 1967. Luther Brewer sold the coupe to Jack Cunningham at mid-season, then built a new car to finish the year as champion car owner. (Luther Brewer collection)

A full house watches as Keith Hightshoe (Larry Swanson 14) dances around the outside of the heat race field at Belleville. Dale Reed (Pius Selenke 43) is at the back of this pack and also thinks the high road is the way to go. Hightshoe won the main event on this day. (L. A. Ward photo)

Gene Gennetten and Bill Rhine's Batmobile combine for more hardware. (Tom Powell photo)

Topeka 1968

Dick Sutcliffe has his Gary Hanna Chevy in victory lane again. It would be nice, however, if Dick would take a cue from his trophy presenter and clean up his boots. (Tom Powell photo)

Eddie Leavitt (Dick Howard 2) shows us what we've suspected all along, none of the Kansas City gang give a hoot about footwear. (Tom Powell photo)

Bill Rigsby (George Hibbs 69) leads Frankie Lies (Kenny Riffle 55) at Belleville. Rigsby survived the afternoon dust storm to take home the winner's check. (Tom Powell photo)

Topeka 1969

Bob Williams wins another trophy dash at Topeka in 1969. "Tiger Bob" had one of the most outstanding seasons in short track history going in his Jack Cunningham Chevy, until his brother, Ken, was killed at Topeka. Typically, Bob was leading the event at the time, but turned his car over to another driver, so he could accompany his brother to the hospital. After several weeks away from the tracks, Williams came back and finished the season the same way he started, by dominating. (Tom Powell photo)

Gary Hanna and Dick Sutcliffe look confident and their hot running black beauty looks ready. These two won everywhere they raced in '69. (Tom Powell photo)

Oren Covert always gave it his best shot on race night in Topeka. (Tom Powell photo)

Topeka 1970

Thad Dosher sits in his championship mount for 1970. This car had a remarkable five year run, it was built by Luther Brewer for Ray Lee Goodwin, who took it to point titles at Olympic and Topeka in '66. Ray Lee was leading Topeka's points (and eventually won) in 1967 when owner Luther Brewer sold it to Jack Cunningham. Cunningham put Dosher in it and won the '67 Knoxville Nationals. Bob Williams started driving it in late '68 and in 1969 Williams was unbeatable with it, winning the points at Knoxville, Topeka, and Olympic. In 1970 Dosher won the Topeka championship and Jayhawk Nationals after Cunningham sold it to Gary Hanna. That's seven point titles and who knows how many wins, with three drivers and three owners! (Leroy Byers photo)

Ken Halteman (13), Jerry "Flea" Atkins (35) and Steve Schultz (Harry Graves 19) skirt around a spinning Russ Hibbard. (Armin Krueger photo)

Jerry Blundy (Mel Moffett 33) sneaks up on the outside of Ron Perkins (Dave Van Patten 19) while Dick Sutcliffe (R & H Farms 40) comes up on the inside. (Ken Simon photo)

Ray Lee Goodwin (Bill Smith 4x) works to stay ahead of Ron Perkins (Van Patten 19), Dale McCarty (Charlie Goodrich 6) and Gene Gennetten (3) at Mid-America. (Armin Krueger photo)

Ed Leavitt (Keith Barker 3) gasses it with Tom Corbin (4) and Sutcliffe (R & H Farms 40) in hot pursuit. (Armin Krueger photo)

Topeka 1971-72

Ray Lee Goodwin gets the hardware for one of his five 1971 wins, at the fairgrounds, with his Charlie Williams & Gary Swenson 24. (Tom Powell photo)

Don Craig led the revitalized super class at Shawnee Speedway by winning six main events and the point title. (Bob Mays collection)

Jay Woodside won the 1972 Mid-America point title after a year long battle with Dick Sutcliffe. Here, Jay is driving his Grant King built, Gary Moulin owned car underneath Roger Larson (Gary Swenson 99) and Ray Lee Goodwin (Williams & Swenson 24) at Lincoln, NE., later that year. (Joe Orth photo)

59

Ralph Parkinson (66) glides on the cushion in his Edmunds sprinter, while Johnny Babb (7) twists his super on the bottom at Knoxville in 1970. (Leroy Byers photo)

Chapter 3
BIRTHPLACE OF THE NATIONALS
KNOXVILLE, IOWA 1958-72

The Marion County Fairgrounds is one of the most famous racing venues in the country now, but in 1958 it was just another dirt track. Marion Robinson carefully massaged the Saturday night show by providing good track conditions night after night and a weekly purse second to none. This brought the out-of-towners, and in 1961 the Nationals. It's interesting to note, that Robinson's first choice for the Nationals was not Knoxville, but Webster City, Iowa! Webster City's fairboard turned him down, so he then went to Knoxville's fairboard with his plan for a big money open competition race and the rest, as they say, is history.

Other tracks in the loop included the Iowa State Fairgrounds in Des Moines (during the fair), Newton, Webster City, Bloomfield and Burlington. Les Turner (1961), Larry Hollingsworth (1961), Brad Teter (1967), Dan Krueger (1967) and Jay Opperman (1970) all lost their lives at the Marion County oval in supers, along with Sonny Helms (1964) at Bloomfield.

Knoxville 1958

Jack Delano (right) shows off Knoxville's first super. It had a Cadillac engine that came out of a hydroplane in Andy Granatelli's garage. (Bob Wilson collection)

Knoxville 1959

Earl Wagner (above) and Slim Gutknecht debuted the "Pink Lady" in 1959, and won their second straight track title. Wagner won 15 mains in those two years and held the track record as well. (Bob Wilson collection)

Dean Sylvester was a top competitor at Knoxville for years. (Bob Wilson collection)

Al DeCarlo, with his coupe, was one of the best Iowa drivers of the 1950's. (Bob Wilson collection)

Danny Richardson's Gold 104's were among the best looking early supers that ran at Knoxville. That is, until meeting with one of the grain bins on Knoxville's backstretch. Although the corn did little damage to Danny's racer, the offended farmer was not happy about the motor oil in his corn flakes. (Bob Wilson collection)

Knoxville 1960

Bill Moyer bought this super-pickup from Bill Smith, of Speedway Motors. He finished eighth in the Knoxville point standings in 1960, but was later almost killed in this car and hung up his goggles in favor of car ownership. (Bob Wilson collection)

Sonny Helms had his sprint car thinly disguised as a supermod. (Bob Wilson collection)

Danny Richardson is rolled up to the line at the Iowa State Fair Championship race in Des Moines. (Bob Wilson collection)

63

Knoxville 1961

Roy Robbins came in from Louisville, KY, to show the Knoxville boys how to use wings to fly. He won the first Knoxville Nationals with ease, using eastern "air scoop" technology previously unknown to the High Plains. In the next few weeks, wings would pop up all over the region. Robbins won over $1200, a sum unheard of for a supermodified race up to that time. (Ed Cole photo)

Knoxville 1962

Bud McCune came up from Brookfield, MO, to win eight features and the 1962 Knoxville point championship. Here, Bud battles fellow Brookfieldian, Bill Pugh. (Bob Wilson collection)

Sonny Helms settles into the Dean Sylvester 12. Helms was a fan favorite who lost his life at Bloomfield, IA, in 1964. (Ed Cole photo)

Knoxville banned wings in 1962, so Kenny Crook came up with this masterpiece. The roof was supposed to emulate an airfoil. It wasn't completely successful. (Bob Wilson collection)

Last Lap - Jerry Richert (Ted Ready 69) holds the groove over Gordon Woolley (Jerry Gilbert 19) on the last lap of the Knoxville Nationals. Woolley was the victim of a loose magneto. While he was trying to hold it in place with one foot and stomp the gas pedal with the other foot, Richert made his move to win the race. (Bob Wilson collection)

Froggy Droz gets ready for work. He was from Radar O'Reilly's hometown of Ottumwa, IA. (Bob Wilson collection)

Angelo Mascaro was a veteran racer from Des Moines. (Bob Wilson collection)

Larry Wilson and his long-nosed beauty, aren't drawing alot of interest. (Bob Wilson collection)

Lloyd Beckman (Bill Smith 4x) leads Earl Wagner (Gutknecht 77) in turn three. (Bob Wilson collection)

Knoxville 1963

At Knoxville, 1963 was Greg Weld's year. Weld completely dominated weekly racing and easily won the 1963 Nationals in his roadster. (Tom Powell photo)

John Babb (21) battles Thad Dosher (Jerry Hayes 11) through turn three. (Bob Wilson collection)

Greg Weld (92) stretches his lead over defending Knoxville Nationals Champ, Jerry Richert (Ready 69). (Bob Wilson collection)

Knoxville 1964

Kenny Weld (Pappy Weld 94) leads Bill Utz (98) and Ken Harper (79). Utz was consistently in the money and as a result, won the points for '64. Weld established himself as a front line driver, in his first full year in supers, by winning the Nationals. (Bob Wilson collection)

NO MORE SPRINT CARS!

Marion Robinson had made sure that no sprint appearing cars were to be allowed through the gates of the Marion County Fairgrounds by outlawing sprint appearing bodies. This rule had been in place since the supers first started showing up in 1958. But for 1964, Robinson went one step further by banning open tube rear ends and requiring cages that were welded to the chassis. The move to enclosed rear ends was seen as a way to save local racers money, while the cage rule was viewed as a safety consideration. Teams were able to circumvent the rear end rule by placing heating duct pipe over the axle, and by 1965 this rule had been scratched from the book. There were still some caged sprints competing, undoubtedly by tack welding or brazing the cages to the frame. In order to run IMCA, all an owner had to do was remove the bolts holding the cage on, then a couple of swift wacks with a good sized hammer and the cage was off! By 1967 Knoxville reversed itself on the welded cage rule as well, approving bolt on cages. At the same time, they also started allowing cars with complete sprint bodies. The moral of this story seems to be, the fewer the rules that racers have to deal with, the fewer the cheaters the promoter has to deal with.

Jerry Blundy is outside his house with his stout as a house #33. (Bob Wilson collection)

Hank Smith clicks off a fast lap at Knoxville. Smith was a regular for years at the Marion County oval, before losing an arm in a 1969 crash. He then became a successful car owner. (Bob Wilson collection)

Knoxville 1965

Jerry Blundy traded in his house on wheels for an honest-to goodness race machine and was repaid with the 1965 Knoxville point championship. The car's name was "Old Blue" and it served Blundy well. Jerry converted it to sprint car configuration in 1968 and won some IMCA races as well as the Sacramento Open, on the big California mile track. (Gene Barnett photo)

Purse Snatcher is what *Hot Rod* magazine called Bob Trostle's creation in their March 1966 issue. Trostle and driver, Johnny Babb certainly did manage to snatch their share of purses at many Midwestern venues. (Bob Wilson collection)

Kenny Weld beat track champ, Jerry Blundy, for the 1965 Nationals crown in Pappy Weld's new super. (Tom Powell photo)

Jay Woodside bought one of the Welds' old supers to run at Knoxville. (Gene Barnett photo)

Knoxville 1966

Sunday afternoon at the Nationals - Rain, in 1966, accounted for the first afternoon race in Nationals history. On the pole, as they head for the green, is Jay Woodside (Ted Hall 9); outside is Ken Weld (Pappy Weld 91); 2nd row, Dick Sutcliffe (Gary Hanna 29) and Jerry Blundy (33). The 3rd row belongs to Ray Lee Goodwin (Luther Brewer 97) and Bob Williams (Weld 24). In the 4th row are, behind the light pole, Earl Wagner (Bill Moyer 81) and Ken Taylor (96). Lloyd Beckman (Charlie Williams & Gary Swenson 124) and Roy Hibbard (Bill Rhine 300) occupy the 5th row. Woodside won over Beckman, Weld and Taylor. Just two weeks after this event, Ken Taylor lost his life in a supermodified race at Marshall, MO. (Craig Agan collection)

Roger Lane (23) scoots out of the picture as Bill Cohee (12), Buddy Taylor (Lowell Carstens 91) and Ray Lee Goodwin (Brewer 97) give chase during the Sunday afternoon National Championship. Despite the dry slick conditions, it was still possible to race three wide on this day. Note the mud piled up on the infield, a result of heavy rain the night before. (Ken Simon photo)

Knoxville 1967

Bill Utz receives a trophy from promoter, Marion Robinson. Utz won his second point title in 1967 with Bill Gault's 98, but was reluctant to defend in '68. Maybe it was the trophy girls? (Bob Wilson collection)

Thad Dosher drove the Jack Cunningham Chevy to a surprise win in the 1967 Nationals, inheriting the lead when Joe Saldana went pitside. Thad also seems concerned about the trophy girl situation. (Beetle Bailey photo)

"Lil' Joe" Saldana was Utz's main antagonist for the '67 point title was. Saldana's radical roadster tore up the black dirt, setting and resetting the one lap track record, finally getting it down to 21.45 seconds on the first night of the Nationals. A broken left rear wheel ruined a certain Nationals win. (Bob Wilson collection)

Al Baldus (36) leads the pack that includes, Phil Reece (47), Lonnie Jensen (7), James Bond (007) and Jay Lyle (83) during a Knoxville heat race. (Beetle Bailey photo)

Dan Krueger (Dick Howard 00) races, just moments before his fatal accident at the 1967 Nationals. Krueger was a well liked newcomer to the racing scene, and his death was taken hard by the Kansas City racing community. (Beetle Bailey photo)

Kansas Citian, Dale Moore backs his Bill Curtis 102 into the third turn fence. (Beetle Bailey Photo)

73

Knoxville 1968

Let's hope Jerry Blundy bought a new helmet for his short caged Mel Moffitt Chevy. (Roger Meier photo)

Ray Lee Goodwin put the Williams & Swenson 24 on the pole for the '68 Nationals, and 30 laps later, into victory lane. (Bob Wilson collection)

It's a sure thing Dick Sutcliffe would have been right at home in the days of wire wheels and cloth helmets. Sutcliffe won Knoxville's point championship in the Gary Hanna mount, and here it seems he is quite pleased with the track's improved trophy girl. Marion Robinson stands ready as a backup if needed. (Bob Wilson collection)

Jerry Blundy (33), Earl Wagner (Moyer 98), Bob Williams (Weld 94) and Dick Sutcliffe (Hanna 29) wage war in turn one. (Bob Wilson collection)

Ken Williams (Ken Stolfus 7) does some fence testing during the Nationals A main. (Beetle Bailey photo)

Lee Kunzman (Mel Moffett 41) struggles to stay ahead of Dick Sutlciffe (Hanna 29). (Bob Wilson collection)

Looks like Don Carlson forgot to stretch his midget when he put his T-body on this beauty at 34 Raceway in Burlington, IA. The way the headers are mounted, it must need to be louder, too! (Roger Meier photo)

Knoxville 1969

1969 Knoxville point winner, "Tiger" Bob Williams (Cunningham 14) pushes his way to the front of another main event against Johnny Babb (Dave Van Patton 19) and Ben Hollifield. (Roger Arndt photo)

Kenny Gritz (Larry Snyder 12) upset the big guns to win the 1969 Knoxville Nationals. Sadly, just 16 days after his victory, he was killed in an IMCA sprint car race in his hometown of Lincoln, NE. (Tom Powell photo)

Jan Opperman came to Knoxville full time in 1969, with Bill Smith's Speedway Motors entry, and impressed most of the railbirds. (Beetle Bailey photo)

Johnny Babb seems happy to get the flag in a Burlington, IA, feature, but his car looks steamed. (Roger Meier photo)

Knoxville 1970

After three straight years as bridesmaid, Joe Saldana finally caught Knoxville's bouquet in 1970. Driving the red deuce for Bill Chadborne & John Leverenz, Joe cleaned house, winning the point title by a mile. He then took the Knoxville Nationals before saying goodbye and heading to USAC. (Leroy Byers photo)

Big Ralph Parkinson (66) always came to Knoxville ready to race. Here he is about to buckle into his semi-downtube Edmunds Chevy, for a run at the Nationals. (Leroy Byers photo)

Sonny Smyser (8) gives Sam Austin (Charlie Schenkel 91) a good look at his right rear. (Leroy Byers photo)

Jay Woodside (Hank Smith 5) carries a slight lead over Dick Sutcliffe (R & H Farms 40) and Roger Larson (Ray Royal 59) as they round Knoxville's fourth bend. (Leroy Byers photo)

J. L. Cooper (Long Chevy 32) battles with Steve Schultz (Jim Mahoney 2) and Dale McCarty (9), during 1970 Knoxville Nationals action. (Leroy Byers photo)

Double dose of Jerrys - The 1962 Knoxville Nationals champion, Jerry Richert (Frank Wagner 63) tries to hold off a surging Jerry Blundy (Mel Moffett 33) during a 1970 Knoxville Nationals race. Blundy snared two feature wins during the season. (Leroy Byers photo)

Arizonan, Bob Moore (Pete Boskens 57), tries to hold off the twin charges of Nebraskan, Ken Parde (95), and Kansan, Jon Backlund (Jack Norris 15) during the 1970 Knoxville Nationals. (Leroy Byers photo)

Steve Ungar goes to full opposite lock trying to get his Myles Engineering Chevy past Bob Williams (Weld 94). (Leroy Byers photo)

Knoxville 1971

Jan Opperman pushes his Cahill Brothers ride to the starting line for the 1971 Knoxville Nationals. Opp fended off heavy pressure from Earl Wagner and Ed Leavitt for the win. (Beetle Bailey photo)

Duane "Stoney" Stoneking was a veteran sprint car racer in the Mississippi Valley area, when he put together this super to run at 34 Raceway in Burlington, IA. (Roger Meier photo)

Steve Schultz bought the 1970 Knoxville championship winning car for 1971. He had several good runs and finished in the top ten in points. (Phil Dullinger photo)

Jerry Blundy just missed another Knoxville point championship in 1971, winning five features and finishing second to Ray Lee Goodwin. Jerry's last year as a Knoxville regular would be 1971. A mid-season crash at Webster City in 1972 caused arm injuries, after which he never recovered his winning style at Knoxville. (Beetle Bailey photo)

Knoxville 1972

Lonnie Jensen (Larry Swanson 14) closes in on Jeff Rice (55) in Knoxville's turn two. Jensen won just once in '72, but finished well often enough for the point championship. (Joe Orth photo)

Mike Thomas raced regularly at Knoxville for years. Although he never won at the Marion County oval, he managed a few wins elsewhere, including a trip to victory lane at Burlington. (Roger Meier photo)

Thad Dosher (R & H Farms 40) splatters mud on Knoxville's famous fence in turn one. The 1967 Knoxville Nationals champ became a force once again in 1972. (Phil Dullinger photo)

Don Schoenfeld, of exhaust header fame, tries to keep his coupe ahead of a fast closing Jack Belk (Al Weiland 37) during an afternoon show at Muskogee in 1968. (Mike Pogue collection)

Chapter 4
RACIN' ON TULSA TIME
TULSA, OKLAHOMA 1960-61, 1966-83

The supermodified history of the Tulsa State Fairgrounds is a unique one. The supers were first tried in 1960, at the fairgrounds, without much success, then came back in 1966 for the long term. Ervin Wolfe was the promoter in '66 until his death in mid-1969. Wolfe's widow, Jackie was then in charge until 1972, when Hugh Finnerty took over.

In 1974 the old fairgrounds track was replaced with a brand new facility built right next door. This new track became a hold-your-breath place for racers and fans alike. In 1979 former racer, Stan Durrett took over promotional control. The Oil Capital Racing Association sanctioned all the weekly racing during the era.

Other tracks in the area included Muskogee, Enid and Bartlesville, in Oklahoma, and Joplin in Missouri. Bill Dillard (1961) and Jim Van Beber (1969) lost their lives on the old Tulsa Speedway while Jeff Sikes (1975), Leonard Perlich (1976), Junior Taft (1981) and Gene Daniel (1981) were victims of the new track.

Tulsa 1960-61

Leroy Ellis ran this car during the 1960 and '61 seasons at Tulsa. The supers, or "bugs" as they were called, were controversial and by 1962, the track had gone back to the full-bodied modifieds. Although the modifieds were considered safer, Ellis lost his life in one in 1965, at Tulsa. (Mike Pogue collection)

85

Tulsa 1966

By 1966, the Tulsa Speedway cars were once again moving towards supermodified configuration. The team of Buddy Cagle (driver), Jack Zink (owner) and Denny Moore (mechanic) built the number 52 car with the frame upside down, and backwards! Here Buddy closes in on Ron Fowler in Al Weiland's coupe. Fowler held Cagle off, frequently enough to claim the championship. (Mike Pogue collection)

Tulsa 1967

Buddy Cagle sits proudly in his new Zink-by-Moore creation for 1967. They went on to dominate the season. (Mike Pogue collection)

Pete York poses with the brand new Del Torrance super. (Mike Pogue collection)

Dan Diaz (63) drives around Bill Crouch (89). "Smilin' Dan" nailed a big win at Muskogee over Buddy Cagle. (Mike Pogue collection)

87

Tulsa 1968

Buddy Cagle swept to championships at Tulsa and Muskogee in 1968 with the Zink Trackburner. (Mike Pogue collection)

Don Nehr (94), Jim Capps (20) and Buddy Cagle (Jack Zink 52) lead the field out of turn four and down the front stretch at Tulsa Speedway. (Mike Pogue collection)

Odell Anderson (30) and Junior Duvall (Charlie Wells 21) battle with Pat Patterson's wedge. (Mike Pogue collection)

Tom Laster ran this old Indy roadster with some very unusual headers. (Mike Pogue collection)

Evard Humphrey (Larry Nailon 12) pushes to stay ahead, while Al Lemmons (Ray Cates 2) pushes to get ahead on Tulsa's cushion. (Mike Pogue collection)

Tulsa 1969

Harold Leep took his Ray Cates Ford to 13 feature wins and the Tulsa track title in 1969, to go along with championships at Wichita and Oklahoma City. (Mike Pogue collection)

Bill Sanders (25) and Jack Belk (88) toss dirt over Muskogee Speedway's wall. After a couple of nasty wrecks, Sanders decided fenders were a better bet and started racing late models, with great success. (Mike Pogue collection)

Bud Hatch (87) has a slight lead over Emmett Hahn (Joe Cox 33) at Ozark Speedway in Joplin, MO. Hatch was a regular at the little quarter mile oval, which featured some great racing. (Mike Pogue collection)

Jackie Howerton in the Del Torrance Ace began pressuring the veterans on a regular basis. (Mike Pogue collection)

Jackie Howerton (Del Torrance 1) has to be wondering where all the offsets came from, as both Buddy Cagle (Zink 52) and Dale McDaniels (Brown, Emmerson, Rutherford & Layne 81) have their seats in far right and low position. Ozark Speedway in Joplin, MO, is the backdrop for this contest. (Mike Pogue collection)

Fred Tullis (Corky Felker 14) pushes to keep his distance from future USAC stock car kingpin, Dean Roper (88) at Joplin. The goofy appearance of Felker's car belies the fact that it was soundly engineered and well built. (Mike Pogue collection)

Tulsa 1970

Angie's Kid - Angelo Howerton was a four-time Tulsa Speedway champion in the 1960's, and his son Jackie started off the 1970's with his own Tulsa title in the Zink 1300. The younger Howerton moved to USAC the next year. (Mike Pogue collection)

Derrill Brazeal (Junior Taft 21) leads Emmett Hahn (Torrance 1) and Chick Shaddox (17). Shaddox won the 1970 championship at Muskogee. (Mike Pogue collection)

D. E. Suggs (16) is chased by Doug Johnson (5) and Mike Jimerson (70). (Mike Pogue collection)

Tulsa 1971

Tom Lambert (93) is chased by the Zink team of Buddy Cagle (52) and Emmett Hahn (1300). (Mike Pogue collection)

A pair of veterans battle at Tulsa Speedway. Junior Taft (22) and D. E. Suggs (Bill Lewis 54) look for the checkered flag. (Mike Pogue collection)

Benny "Wahoo" Taylor (13) pressures Mike Jimerson (70) as they round the curve at Tulsa Speedway. Taylor won "Best Engineered Car" for this ride, which he designed and built. (Mike Pogue collection)

Jack Layne (Melvin Jarnagin 44) tries to hold off a charging James Eubanks (Cox 33). Eubanks was voted "Most Improved Driver" at Tulsa in 1971. (Mike Pogue collection)

Tulsa 1972

Vic Paddock (73) tries to stave off the challenges of Emmett Hahn (Zink 01). Hahn won the first of his five Tulsa Speedway championships in 1972. (Tim Malone photo)

Ray Crawford (James Plunkett 64) has a slight lead on Derrill Brazeal (Taft 21) and Doug Johnson (35). (Tim Malone photo)

Tulsa 1973

Emmett Hahn won nine features and his second Tulsa championship in a row aboard the John Zink 52, in 1973. (Tim Malone photo)

George Armstrong had his best season yet, hauling down three wins aboard the Paul Cunningham 8. (Tim Malone photo)

"Little Joe" Siefried (Gene Holoman 74) pushes hard to stay in front of Junior Taft (22). (Tim Malone photo)

97

Tulsa 1974

Al Lemmons (Wayne Wisley 19), Derrill Brazeal (Taft 21) and John Shipley (90) all think they know where the fast groove is. Brazeal for sure did, as he won the Tulsa points in 1974. (Tim Malone photo)

Larry Ring tried hard with his under funded team. (Tim Malone photo)

Long time fan favorite, veteran Al Lemmons had some good runs in the Wayne Wisley 19. (Tim Malone photo)

Little Big Man - Mike McGee was able to overcome his physical limitations to become a tough racer at Tulsa. His car, owned and built by his father, Phil, won the "Best Engineered" award at Tulsa Speedway in 1974. (Tim Malone photo)

Tulsa 1975

Derrill Brazeal (Taft 21) and teammate/owner Junior Taft (22) charge over the Tulsa Speedway clay. (Tim Malone photo)

Jeff Sikes (99) puts a move on Larry Madden (Aaron Madden 1). On June 7, 1975, Sikes lost his life in a B feature crash at Tulsa. (Tim Malone photo)

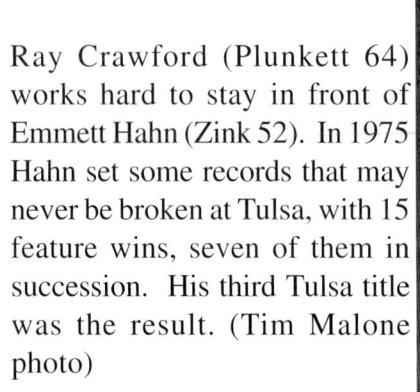

Ray Crawford (Plunkett 64) works hard to stay in front of Emmett Hahn (Zink 52). In 1975 Hahn set some records that may never be broken at Tulsa, with 15 feature wins, seven of them in succession. His third Tulsa title was the result. (Tim Malone photo)

Tulsa 1976

Ray Crawford piloted the beautiful Harold Hillenberg piece to his first Tulsa Speedway crown in 1976, picking up seven main event wins en route. (Tim Malone photo)

Tulsa 1977

For the Tulsa wars, Jay Woodside had this good looking mount provided by Paul Harrington. (Tim Malone photo)

Tulsan, Mike McClelland, did not win any "most popular driver" awards, but he won races. (Tim Malone photo)

Terry Colvin (90) races with Jerry Stone (Jelly Wilhelm 24), while Junior Taft (22) creeps up on the inside. Taft would end up a victim of the big track at Tulsa, in 1981, precipitating the mandatory use of wings from then on. (Tim Malone photo)

Tulsa 1978

Emmett Hahn won nine races and his fifth Tulsa crown in 1978. Hahn, along with chief mechanic, Denny Moore, crew chief, Herschel Goodnight and his Zink crew set new standards at which future generations would shoot with records for most wins in a season, most consecutive wins and career wins. Jack Zink is, perhaps, the only car owner in this book to go from Indy cars and end up with Supermodifieds. He owned the winning cars in both the 1955 (Bob Swiekert) and 1958 (Pat Flaherty) Indy 500s and continued to own Indy cars through the 1967 season. (Tim Malone photo)

Tulsa 1979-80

George Armstrong (Crain & Thurman 1) prepares for battle on the Tulsa frontstretch. Armstrong won his first Tulsa Speedway championship in 1979. (Mike Monatoboy photo)

Derrill Brazeal (Lloyd K. Stephens 21) suffered career ending injuries when a track packing vehicle tangled with his OFIXCO Special. (Mike Monatoboy photo)

Tulsa 1981-83

Second generation ace, Donnie Crawford (Harold Hillenberg 56) presses Bob Ewell (Ry-son 85) in Tulsa Speedway action. The young Crawford came out of the micro-midget ranks to team with his father, three-time Tulsa champion, Ray Crawford, in 1982, winning his second time out. In 1983, Donnie won twice, and grabbed his first championship ring. With that title, he became the last supermodified champion on the great plains. (John Parham photo)

Harold Leep (Pat Suchy 76) looks cool and calm, while Rick Salem (22) charges underneath him. The action was at 81 Speedway early in the 1979 season. (Jerry Leep photo)

Chapter 5
81 & COUNTING
WICHITA, KANSAS 1962-81

Eighty-One Speedway, in Wichita, actually had two eras of supermodified racing. The first 1962-67 was when they adopted Kansas City rules for the class (i.e. short wheel base, no starters), then in 1968 went with the rules coming out of Oklahoma City, (long wheel base, starters etc).

Bill Hall oversaw operations then; his son, C. Ray, does today. The Hall family is one of the few promoters of supers represented in this book, who is still promoting the same track in the new millennium. Arnold Horner (1979) was the only man to die in a supermodifed at 81 Speedway.

Wichita 1962-65

Veteran Wichita campaigner, Walt McWhorter, built this piece for less than $100! By the way, it won its first time out. (Ken Greteman photo)

Texan, Cotton Farmer, was the first out-of-towner to win at Eighty-One in 1965. He did it in the "Blue Lady" owned by Larry North. By the looks of this car's hood, there is a 1962 or '63 Chevy Bel-Air missing it's front fenders. (Ken Greteman photo)

Bill Nelson (Bob Garner 15) seems a little light in the front, while the guy in front is a little heavy in the left rear. Harold Leep, 1965-66-67 Eighty-One Speedway champ, is glad his Jelly Wilhelm 99 can skirt to the outside. (Ken Greteman photo)

The Big Wheel - Action at 81 Speedway could get wild at times. If you didn't have a tight grip on your steering wheel, you could find yourself griping someone's front wheel! This shot is from around 1962. (Ken Greteman photo)

Ray Riner gets ready to show his fins to the other drivers. (Ken Greteman photo)

Owner LaVern Nance, looks quite happy with his brand new super, while its driver, Grady Wade, looks anxious to get into the seat. (Ken Greteman photo)

Wichita 1966

Grady Wade proved to be a winner when he stepped into the Chet Wilson "Offy Killer". (Ken Greteman photo)

Frank Offutt looks friendly from his Friendly Chevrolet in the 81 pits. Let's hope he checked the rear end grease before he went out. (Ken Greteman photo)

Bill Nelson and car owner "Georgia Bob" Garner made a tough combination even tougher when they found nothing in the rules forbidding wings. Their advantage only lasted a few weeks before track management sent the rule book back for a revised printing. (Ken Greteman photo)

Another tough Texan who came to 81 was Billy Joe Smith, from Amarillo. (Ken Greteman photo)

Wichita 1967

Roy Bryant (Red Forshee 84), Harold Leep (Wilhelm 99), Jay Woodside (Ted Hall 9), Frankie Lies (Jack Walker & Kenny Riffle 53) and Al Murie (11) prepare to receive the green. Leep won the 81 point title in 1967 for the third year running. (Ken Greteman photo)

Roy Bryant found victory lane several times in Red Forshee's 84. (Ken Greteman photo)

Frank Lies almost looks too big for his supermodified, which is owned by Jack Walker and Kenny Riffle. (Ken Greteman photo)

By the looks of the roll cage on Billy Jack Casper's Gunter Signs Special, the city park may be short one picnic table! (Ken Greteman photo)

Wichita 1968

Underrated Walt McWhorter won the 81 Speedway point title in 1968, along with the Kansas State Championship at Hutchinson. Walt built and owned his own cars. (Ken Greteman photo)

Pinky Mullen gives his Charlie Turpin 02 a hug before heading out to another 81 Speedway payday. (Ken Greteman photo)

Bill Curless stands at attention beside his sedan, owned by his brother, Carl. (Ken Greteman photo)

Doc Lamb (7) has a slight lead on Francis Hoppensteadt (18), while rookie, Jerry Stone (M. C. Stone 5), pokes his nose in on the action. (Ken Greteman photo)

111

Wichita 1969

Harold Leep teamed with Tulsan Ray Cates, in 1969 and they had a dream season together. His fourth 81 Speedway supermodified championship was the result. (Ken Greteman photo)

Paul Dutton and his crew look confident about their prospects in 1969. (Ken Greteman photo)

Journeyman Wichita racer, Kenny Myers poses for the lensman. (Ken Greteman photo)

Youngster, Jerry Stone, seems to be wondering what he can do to make his M. C. Stone 5 more competitive against 81's veterans. (Ken Greteman photo)

Wichita 1970

Grady Wade relaxes with the Pat Suchy Transmission Service Special. (Mar-Car photo)

Frank Lies (Riffle 55) beat out Forest Coleman and Walt McWhorter for the 1970 title at 81 Speedway and won the K. O. Christian Memorial race along the way. (Mike Pogue collection)

Herb Copeland (Evart Isaac 8) looks focused before 81 Speedway hotlaps. (Ken Greteman photo)

Wichita 1971

Dave Ross looks apprehensive about his supermodified career winding down in 1971. It would be Dave's last full year in supers. (Jerry Leep photo)

Wichita 1972-73

Dale Reed (Evart Isaac 6) won his second consecutive 81 Speedway title in 1972 ahead of Grady Wade, Walt McWhorter, and teammate, Herb Copeland. In '73 he made it three straight, this time over Copeland, Larry Dewell, McWhorter and Jim Harkness. (Jerry Leep photo)

Wichita 1974-75

81 Speedway shut down the weekly supermodified show in 1974, but realized they needed the supers, and brought them back in 1975. Roy Bryant (Harold Sparks 37) roars around the outside of the pack which includes Frank Lies (56), Dale Reed (Isaac 6), Lonnie Snowden (99) and Harold Leep (Wilhelm 24). Bryant passed these guys often enough to win his first 81 Speedway championship in 1975. (Jerry Leep photo)

Roy Bryant (Sparks 37) leads Roger Thompson (John Schippert 4), Mike Peters (Norman Gum 71) and Bob McCutchen (77) on 81's heavy clay. (Jerry Leep photo)

Wichita 1976

Jerry Stone (Shot Hampton 94) drives under Jay Woodside (Wilhelm 24) and Roy Bryant (Sparks 37) during the early laps of an 81 Speedway main event. (Jerry Leep photo)

Terry Brown (8), Gordon Lucas (Les Steinert 5) and Wylan Cattrell (14) search for the fastest groove. (Jerry Leep photo)

Wichita 1977

The Chet Wilson Memorial was run in 1977 at 81 Speedway to honor the Wichita racing legend who had recently passed away. Driving for Chet's son, Jerry Wilson, Jay Woodside pulled down one of the biggest wins of his career in the inaugural event. (Warren Vincent photo)

Herb Copeland (Poor Boys Racing Team 15) and Roger Thompson (Schippert 4) glide across the 81 clay. (Jerry Leep photo)

Jim Selenke (43), another son of a famous Wichita car owner, Pius Selenke, tries to hold off the charge of Bill Nichols (3). (Jerry Leep photo)

Perennial challenger, Jerry Everhart (Issac 8), is introduced to the crowd. (Warren Vincent photo)

Wichita 1978

Walt McWhorter (98) won his third 81 title in a row, in 1978, and fourth overall. Chasing the Wichita veteran is young Mike Peters (Gum 71). (Jerry Leep photo)

Dale Reed (Isaac 6) has the inside line, as Fred Hembree (79) pushes his slight advantage. (Jerry Leep photo)

Bob Hurley (04) strains to stay ahead of Mike Peters (Gum 71) and Jerry Stone (Wilhelm 24). (Jerry Leep photo)

Wichita 1979

Dale Reed capped a great season, in 1979, with the 81 Speedway championship driving the Chet Wilson Racing Engines Special, owned by Jerry Wilson. (Jerry Leep photo)

Darrell Bybee (9) glides on the cushion, while Wylan Cattrell (14) power slides to the inside. (Jerry Leep photo)

Harold Leep brought out Lonnie Snowden's "Missile" and promptly torpedoed the wall. (Jerry Leep photo)

Ace Gearhart (is that a great name for a race driver or what?) has Court Grandstaff (9x) creeping up on the outside at 81 Speedway. Court is now a successful sprint car owner. (Jerry Leep photo)

Jeff Forshee (Pete Forshee 3) joines a mess in progress, but is still trying to keep the cage side up. (Jerry Leep photo)

Dale Reed (Wilson 25) and Jon Johnson (Ray Charles & Johnson 86) battle in another 81 Speedway A main. (Jerry Leep photo)

Wichita 1980-81

Jeff Forshee (P. Forshee 3) keeps the inside line from Dale Looper (90). (Jerry Leep photo)

Terry Uehling straps into his Trade Winds Special before an 81 hot lap session. (Jerry Leep photo)

Rick Riner had his great looking Dave Moore built car ready to go. (Jerry Leep photo)

Harold Leep (Snowden 99) blasts into turn three, while Jim Selenke (43) plays it straight in the high groove. (Jerry Leep photo)

Kenny Gritz (12) races with Frank Brennfoerder (Brennfoerder & Duane Starr 5) through turn one at Eagle in 1968. Gritz's bright future was snuffed out by a fatal sprint car crash at the Nebraska State Fairgrounds in 1969. (Leroy Byers photo)

Chapter 6
HUSKER HEROS
LINCOLN, NEBRASKA 1964-74

There were several tracks in the Lincoln loop at the beginning of the supermodified era, starting with Midwest Speedway and Eagle Race way. Jerry Gerdes and Jerry Biskup were the promoters at Midwest, before giving way to Pete Liekam. Harvey Kropp built Eagle and ran things there.

Midwest and Eagle either co-produced or fought over Lincoln's premier racing attraction throughout the 1960's and 1970's, with sanctioning by the Nebraska Modified Racing Association.

In 1967, the Blue Valley Racing Association allowed supermodifieds at their shows in Fairbury and Beatrice. The Nebraska State Fairgrounds in Lincoln hosted some super shows as did Sunset Speedway in Omaha. There were no fatalities during the supermodified era at any Lincoln area tracks.

The "Roarin' Rebel" Roy McCain guided his Guy Hollamon owned piece to victory lane often. He won the Nebraska Modified Racing Association championship in 1963 and was second in '64. (Gene Barnett photo)

Lincoln 1964

Lloyd Beckman (Bill Smith 4x) was another guy that had no trouble finding victory lane in 1964. Lloyd easily outdistanced everyone for the crown that year, winning five times at Midwest Speedway, and seven times at Eagle. (Tom Powell photo)

125

Lincoln 1965

A good crowd watches the supers thunder down the main stretch at the Nebraska State Fairgrounds. Willie Hecke (5) leads Wayne Luginbill (17) and the rest of the pack. (Bob Mays collection)

Kenny Gritz (12) does his level best to hold off Lloyd Beckman (B. Smith 4x) at Midwest. (Gene Barnett photo)

Wayne Rutland chauffeured the Ray Royal entry to one feature win in '65. (Gene Barnett photo)

Don Droud (9) has both feet on the brakes trying to stop short of Wayne Luginbill (17) in his "Flinstone Flyer." Ed Bowes (54) cruises past thinking "three's a crowd." (Gene Barnett photo)

Lincoln 1966

Lloyd Beckman (Charlie Williams & Gary Swenson 24) owned the 1966 season at Midwest Speedway, at one point winning 10 features in a row! He more than doubled the point total of the second place man. (Gene Barnett photo)

Frank Brennfoerder ran consistently in his CAE rig, and he's one of the all-time nice guys in the sport. (Gene Barnett photo)

Keith Hightshoe came out, in Ed Smith's pretty job, to snag a couple of main events at Midwest. (Gene Barnett photo)

Leon Lahodny drove hard and won some hardware. (Gene Barnett photo)

Lincoln 1967

Denny Oltman was one of the top wheelmen of the Blue Valley Racing Association at Beatrice and Fairbury. (Don McChesney collection)

Mark Crear (Ira Schrieber 67) had some strong runs in '67. The promising young racer lost his life in a motorcycle crash in 1968. (Gene Barnett photo)

Lonnie Jensen (Fred Goodrich 67) stands on the right front as Bob Scanlon (3) sneaks by. (Gene Barnett photo)

Lincoln 1968

WE'RE NOT GONNA TAKE IT!

Labor unrest has punctuated Lincoln's racing community during virtually every era. On July 4, 1958, the modified drivers at Capitol Beach Speedway went on strike over the purse and closed down the track for the remainder of the year. After that, all seemed well and good until just before the start of the 1968 season. The Nebraska Modified Racing Association went to Jerry Gerdes and Jerry Biskup, the owners of Midwest Speedway, and demanded an increase in the purse. Midwest played to huge crowds ever since it's opening in 1963 but, never-the-less, Gerdes and Biskup were in financial trouble. They said no, so the NMRA moved to Eagle Raceway for the 1968 season and the fans followed, for the most part. Midwest continued with supers in 1968, but with a 305 c.i. limit similar to the tracks in Central Nebraska. Both tracks had huge car counts during the season, but Eagle won the war with the fans. In 1974 there were more problems and the NMRA took its show back to Midwest Speedway. In mid-1975 the NMRA was back at Eagle, but car counts were only averaging in the high-teens. By 1977 there was no weekly open wheel racing in Lincoln. The 1980's saw the beginning of a new era of racing in Lincoln, with the emergence of 360 sprints. Alas, this too has been threatened with another dispute between the driver's association and promoters in 2000. It seems that the only thing these disputes have taught us, is that no matter who wins, the fans always lose.

Four Wide! - Roger Rager (2) wings it down low, while Rich Brahmer (Larry Upton 1), Rex Jordan (Sam Holliman 19) and Leon Lahodny (George Bogue & Don Melton 96) cover the rest of the surface at Eagle Raceway. (Leroy Byers photo)

Midwest lost the locals in a purse dispute, but the 1968 season was not short on thrills. Here, Wayne Holz (73), Dave Milbourn (53), Dean Burling (74), Willie Hecke (John Davisson 1) and Russ Brahmer (Leroy Kallweit 55) battle for the top spot. (George Edeal photo)

Harold Leep (Jelly Wilhelm 99) tore up Eagle Raceway in 1968, winning six out of nine features he contested and just being nosed out for the point title by Lloyd Beckman. There's a story of Leep quitting a car owner because the owner refused to pay Leep 50%, instead of the standard 40%. Harold then jumped into Wilhelm's car. The previous car owner walked up to Jelly, during a race that Leep was leading, and asked Wilhelm if he was paying Harold 50%. "I'd rather pay him 50%, than pay someone 40% to chase him," was Jelly's response. Here, Leep battles with Gene Gennetten (Bill Rhine 300) at the Amarillo Speed Bowl in Texas. (Leroy Byers photo)

Lincoln 1969

Roy McCain (Hollamon 75) has George Hite (Lonnie Morosic 9) on the inside as they maneuver Eagle's high banks. (Leroy Byers photo)

Jim Heble (7) tries to hold on while Jim Riggins (11) comes up on the outside. (Leroy Byers photo)

Jim Van Sickle (21) hangs onto his position, as Leon Lahodny (Bogue & Melton 96) mounts a challenge. (Leroy Byers photo)

Eddie Bowes started running with the front pack in his brand new Ray Royal four-bar. (Leroy Byers photo)

Lincoln 1970

Ray Lee Goodwin has a determined look on his face as he sits behind the wheel of the Williams & Swenson Chevy. Goodwin won seven features at Eagle on his road to the championship. (Leroy Byers photo)

Lonnie Jensen combined consistent finishes with three feature wins, in his Larry Swanson entry, to nail down his first Beatrice point title in 1970. (Leroy Byers photo)

Ed Bowes (Ray Royal 57) keeps Roger Rager (Larry Snyder 1) and Jan Opperman (B. Smith 4x) lined up behind him. (Leroy Byers photo)

133

Dan Holliman (Holliman 19), Larry Upton (Eldon Thomas 30), Lonnie Jensen (Swanson 14), Del Schmidt (Dale Rumsey 11) and Joe Saldana (Bill Chadborne & John Leverenz 2) each have their own opinion about the fast groove at Eagle. (Leroy Byers photo)

Frank Brennfoerder (Wes Vandervoort 26) races in tight quarters with "Buddy Parker." The Parker name was a pseudonym for Ralph Parkinson, Jr. The young Parkinson would use it whenever he wanted to avoid scrutiny from the IMCA, which frowned on its drivers running non-sanctioned races. (Leroy Byers photo)

Dan Holliman (Holliman 19) has his hands full with Louie Quatrocchi (18) and Frank Brennfoerder (Vandervoort 26). (Leroy Byers photo)

Jan Opperman (B. Smith 4x) saddles up. Sitting on the trailer in front of the car is Jerry (Yogi) Janssen, who was responsible for bringing Opperman to the Midwest in 1968. (Leroy Byers photo)

Lonnie Jensen (Swanson 14), Ralph Blackett (Snyder 1) and Ray Lee Goodwin (Williams & Swenson 24) demonstrate three perfect power slides at Eagle. Blackett's season started fast, with a dominating win at Beatrice, and ended early with a broken arm at Knoxville. (Leroy Byers photo)

Car owner, Ed Smith (left) keeps both hands on his wallet, while his driver, "Honest Al" Murie surveys the competition. Known in some circles as "Big Al," Murie was one of the legendary drivers to come out of the Kansas City area. It seems everyone I've talked to for this book, has an Al Murie story. Al made the 1970 Knoxville National A main driving for Smith. The car is the former Les Vaughn Offy that A. J. Foyt took to his first big win in 1956 at Fargo, ND. (Leroy Byers photo)

This turn three traffic jam at Eagle includes Vince Kelly (Eldon Rhoten, Jim Golden & Kelly 23), Keith Hightshoe (Ernie DiCroce 4), Denny Oltman (M. E. Dole 77) and Stan Borofsky (92). Note Borofsky's choice of driving attire; we had no idea Simpson made flame retardant T-shirts! (Leroy Byers photo)

Lincoln 1971

Lloyd Beckman dominated Eastern Nebraska in 1971, winning both the Eagle and Beatrice points. Here he is climbing in the Bill Smith Chevy, at Eagle. (Bob Mays collection)

Jon Backlund keeps his former Joe Saldana roadster, now owned by Jim Mahoney, in front of Californian, Curt Waters (E. Smith 44). (Leroy Byers photo)

Dan Holliman (Holliman 19) sticks a wheel into Jim Heble (7). (Beetle Bailey photo)

Lonnie Morosic stuck with his rear engine Plymouth for driver, George Hite. (Leroy Byers photo)

Lincoln 1972

Lloyd Beckman (B. Smith 4x) and Lonnie Jensen (Swanson 14) battled hard and fast for the point crown at Eagle in 1972. Beckman set a record for consecutive wins, with four, but Jensen won more races more often, and was on top of the points at the end. (Leroy Byers photo)

Herb Heckman (3), Dutch Buettenbach (9) and Rod Knoedler (5) look for the magic that will make them the quickest through Eagle's turn one. (Joe Orth photo)

139

Jim Golden (Rhoten, Golden, & Kelly 27) runs his Kurtis Indy roadster past Keith Hightshoe (Lyle Sinner 6) and Danny Holliman (Holliman 19). (Butch Bahr photo)

Roger Larson (Gary Swenson 99) was an up-and-comer, who won his first feature at Eagle in 1972. (Joe Orth photo)

Dick Sutcliffe (Dave Van Patten 19) watches Eddie Leavitt's (E. Smith 44) line on the back stretch. (Joe Orth photo)

Jim Riggins (Arnie Rudder 8) strains to stay ahead, as Thad Dosher (Gary Hanna 29) strains to stay out of the infield. (Joe Orth photo)

Lincoln 1973

Lonnie Jensen (E. Smith 44) leads Don Droud (2) in Eagle's second turn. Jensen took the point title with three wins. (Joe Orth photo)

Don Maxwell (R. D. Bisping 00) came from Albuquerque, NM, to start a car building business in Lincoln. He also drove a little, almost winning the championship in '73. (Joe Orth photo)

Ed Leavitt jumped into Bill Smith's 4x and broke Joe Saldana's three year old track record with a 15.07 second lap. (Joe Orth photo)

Merlin Peterson (7) struggles to pass a wingless Herb Heckman (3). (Joe Orth photo)

Lincoln 1974

Mr. Excitement - Dick Sutcliffe looks ready to go hotlapping at Sunset Speedway in Omaha. Dick won three times at Midwest Speedway plus the Sunset special for the '74 season championship in the Bob Trostle wrenched, Dave Van Patten Chevy. (Joe Orth photo)

Jim Golden (Rhoten, Golden, & Kelly 27) and Lonnie Jensen (Swanson 14) go at it in tight quarters at Midwest. (Joe Orth photo)

Gary Dunkle (34) battles with "Ralphie the Racer" Blackett (Jim Springer 28) in a turn one conflict. (Joe Orth photo)

Rex "the Flying" Nun slides his supermodified into Midwest Speedway's first turn. (Joe Orth photo)

Butch Bahr (25) navigates his Bullet Racing Special on the cushion, while Del Schmidt handles the Dale Rumsey Chevy through turn two at Midwest. (Joe Orth photo)

Ken Hoover (19) pushes his supermod past Bob O'Neil's hulking sedan at the Lincoln County Raceway in North Platte, NE, as the 1968 season commences. (George Edeal photo)

Chapter 7
SMALL TOWN THUNDER
CENTRAL NEBRASKA 1967-78

There was no one dominant track in this area, but there was a great circuit consisting of anywhere from two to five tracks at any given time. Hastings, Kearney and Columbus were there at first, along with North Platte. Norfolk and Doniphan and several others then joined the mix. Tracks paid next to nothing but provided some intense competition between drivers and owners who were largely unknown outside the imediate area.

One by one, tracks either dropped the supers, or dropped racing altogether. By 1977 only Doniphan remained and they dropped open wheel cars after the 1978 season. None of the Central Nebraska tracks recorded a fatality during the supers' reign.

Central Nebraska 1967

The Mighty Mouse - Willie Hecke and John Davisson's "Mighty Mouse," were a heavy favorite whenever they pulled into a track. Hecke won the points at Kearney, Hastings and Columbus in 1967 with this coupe; then Davisson built a supermodified and won them all again in '68! (George Edeal photo)

145

Milo Stodola (31) exits the scene as Jim Stewart (88) reverses his momentum. Don Smith (18) watches from the high groove. (George Edeal photo)

Omaha's Dave Milbourn was a rough tough competitor. He won several features at Columbus. (George Edeal photo)

Dave Jolly (16) wants Don Maurer (35) to go on the inside, but Maurer wants to check the air pressure in that left rear. Jolly won twice at Hastings in '67. (George Edeal photo)

Ron Stadeskev (72x), Ray Haase (96) and Lyle Roucha (49) look for running room at Skylark Speedway in Columbus. (George Edeal photo)

Ed Walther (94) and Larry Penrod (39) work Skylark's outside groove, while Wendell Cummings (32) scoots by. Cummings took three flags at Skylark, then retired. (George Edeal photo)

Central Nebraska 1968

Tom Egan (2) and Larry Penrod (39) slide their cars across Kearney's dry slick. (George Edeal photo)

Duane Bender (25) and Roger Abbott (23) look for the fast lane at Skylark. Abbott scored at Columbus and Hastings. (George Edeal photo)

Lynn Grabill (12), Jim Stewart (Fred Garbers 69), Dave Milbourn (53) and Ray Weber (87) hammer away at Columbus. (George Edeal photo)

Lyle Roucha (49) rings every ounce of sidebite out of his coupe, while Russ Brahmer (Leroy Kallweit 55) takes it easy in his supermod at Hastings. Brahmer scored four wins and Roucha managed one in his behemoth. (George Edeal photo)

Central Nebraska 1969

Wilber Hecke stands with the newest edition of the "Mighty Mouse." John Davisson built the motors, Homer Macklin tuned the chassis and Hecke kissed the trophy girls - lots of them. (George Edeal photo)

It's the calm before the storm and Larry Penrod anticipates bad weather for this Hastings race. (George Edeal photo)

Ron Williams got some kisses, too. (George Edeal photo)

Jerry Bell and the Ron Miller & Gay Moon crew look like they could use a good finish. (George Edeal photo)

Don Smith (Marv Dickenson 22) decides to groove Don Maurer's (35) left rear at Kearney. (George Edeal photo)

Willie Hecke (Davisson 1) punts Jerry Bell (50) into Hastings' boondocks. Despite a hard landing, Bell and the car survived. (George Edeal photo)

Dean Ward (Garbers 69) gets a late arriving trophy, while Chuck Sears steadies the flag. The Ward/Garbers combo started late, but finished strong. (George Edeal photo)

Dapper Duane Bender unloads his potent 289 c.i. Ford super before the festivities get started at Kearney. (Duane Bender collection)

Central Nebraska 1970

Don Kissenger can't wait to get his CAE rig off the trailer before mounting up at Hastings. We're sure that wing kept him nailed to the track! (George Edeal photo)

Digging for home is Stan Haack (21) with Jim Adler (Red Aldrich 2) in pursuit. (George Edeal photo)

Pete Peterson (Mel Lammers 5) chases Jack Evans (6) at Kearney. (George Edeal photo)

This Kearney traffic jam includes Ray Mickelson (52), Phil Simmons (75), Gary Gillespy (76), Willie Hecke (Bob Strong 1), Larry Penrod (outside) and Bill Fann (39). (George Edeal photo)

Jack Evans (6) now is being chased by Stan Haack (21) through Kearney's third turn. Evans managed one win at the Buffalo County oval. (George Edeal photo)

Duane Bender (25) goes into the spin cycle and Cliff "Grandstand" Doiel (Louis Grein 3) does a brake check at Kearney. (George Edeal photo)

Homer Macklin seems to be softening up to an enemy agent sent to find out the "Mighty Mouse's" speed secrets. (George Edeal photo)

Cliff "Grandstand" Doiel gets a new Kearney Raceway jacket for copping the main event. His sedan won many events on the west coast in the hands of Jimmy Gordon, before being purchased by the Louis Grein Motor Co. and coming to the Midwest. (George Edeal photo)

Central Nebraska 1971

Willie Hecke (Bob Strong 1) gave every one a high mark at which to shoot. Here he is at Kearney Raceway, where he won his fifth straight point title in 1971. (George Edeal photo)

Bob O'Neil's (Ray Gillen 69) roadster holds the line against Larry Gosnell (77) at Kearney. (George Edeal photo)

Boog - Gerald Bruggeman had R. D. Bisping's 00 racer on the top of the heap at Columbus, easily winning the track title. (Gerald Bruggeman collection)

Chuck Kidwell pushed Ron Fetger's supermodified to a Kearney trophy dash win. They both seem to like the new flagman. (George Edeal photo)

Central Nebraska 1972

Doug Reidy (Aldrich 2) rides the high groove, while Jim Goettsche (Ken Gappa & Goettsche 17) tests the bottom at the brand new Mid-Continent Raceways in Doniphan. Goettsche won the first feature at the new track, then held off Dean Ward for the point title. (Butch Bahr photo)

Bill Fann (Ted Miller 41) runs tight against Jerry Suhr, on the outside. Suhr won championships at Riviera Raceway in Norfolk in 1970-71 and 1973. (Butch Bahr photo)

Lynn Grabill (Lammers 5) tries to hold back the charging hordes, which includes Frank Brennfoerder (Bob Rosso, Ron Alexander & Mike Phillips 14), George Pontious (3) and Ken McCarty (95). (Frank Brennfoerder collection)

Bob O'Neil (Gillen 69) has a slight lead over Jim Adler (Dick Winklebauer 44) and Ken McCarty (95). (Jerry Holmes collection)

Bill Fann (Miller 41) is about to get a free chassis realignment from Wilber Hecke (Howard Carrico 1), Ken McCarty (95) and Don Maurer (35). (Butch Bahr photo)

Lynn Grabill (George Pontious 3) and Ron Williams (29) get ready to entertain another big crowd at Hastings. Note the fire extinquisher behind Grabill's right shoulder. (Butch Bahr photo)

Central Nebraska 1973

Dean Ward and his team pose at Mid-Continent, where Dean took his Don Wilson and Mel Earnest/Nance rig to the 1973 point crown. This car was perhaps the only supermodified powered by a Rambler (a/k/a AMC) engine to ever win a championship. (Butch Bahr photo)

Jim Adler (44) noses into Frank Brennfoerder (Rosso, Alexander & Phillips 14), who noses into Ray Mickelson (52). Gene Brudigan (95) does his best to keep his nose clean. (Frank Brennfoerder collection)

Car owner, Melvin Perry and his driver/son Wendell were regulars at Hastings. (Butch Bahr photo)

Jim Goettsche (Gappa & Goettsche 17) dives inside of Dean Ward (Wilson & Earnest 33) at Mid-Continent. (Butch Bahr photo)

Central Nebraska 1974

Gerald Bruggeman makes sure his motor is in tip top shape on his way to six feature wins and the 1974 Riviera Racway title. "Boog" also won three supermodified point titles in a row at Huset's Speedway in Sioux Falls, SD, 1977-78-79. (Jerry Jacobs photo)

Rookie Mike Haberer (Jerry Holmes 8) prepares to sling mud. (Jerry Jacobs photo)

Getting ready for action at Hastings are, Lynn Grabill (Lammers 5), Wendell Perry (Melvin Perry 72), Ron Williams (Williams & Jim Ellett 29), Don Weyhrich ($1.98), Roger Sundquist (7) and Gene Brudigan (95). (Jerry Jacobs photo)

Central Nebraska 1975

1975 Mid-Continent champ, Ken McCarty, puts his Mel Earnest 11 through its paces. (Jerry Jacobs photo)

Lonnie Morosic brought his rear engine Plymouth to Mid-Continent several times with Ray Flanagan at the controls. (L. A. Ward photo)

Harold Brudigan wants to get his wing just right before going out for hot laps. (Jerry Jacobs photo)

The Norfolk boys came to Mid-Continent in force with Lyle Weyhrich (nearest to the camera), brother Don ($1.98) and Gary Stone (81) lining the pits. (Jerry Jacobs photo)

Central Nebraska 1976

Don Weyhrich ($1.98) leads Willie Hecke (Carrico 1) and Doug Reidy (Lammers 5). Weyhrich swept the honors by winning both Riviera and Mid-Continent point titles in '76. (Jerry Jacobs photo)

Lyle Weyhrich stands on it down the backstretch, in his beautiful coupe. (Jerry Jacobs photo)

Mike Haberer (Holmes 8) gets all crossed up trying to stay with Ray Haase (02). Ray's brother, Bob Haase, is the promoter of Riviera Raceway in Norfolk. (Jerry Jacobs photo)

Central Nebraska 1977

Hard-charging Kim Lingenfelter (Garbers 69) was a threat to win every time he fired the car up in 1977. (Jerry Jacobs photo)

Ray Haase's Southside Salvage Special must be ready to go. (Jerry Jacobs photo)

Cutting a fast lap is Don Smith in his good looking 100-incher. (Jerry Jacobs photo)

Hoskins, NE, resident, Gerald Bruggeman, had a good season at Mid-Continent Speedway, but he made his real mark by winning the first of three Huset's Speedway (Brandon, SD) championships in 1977. (Gerald Bruggeman collection)

162

Central Nebraska 1978

Don Smith (18), Don Vonderfecht (65), Gene Brudigan (95) and Don Weyhrich ($1.98) lineup for the dash. Weyhrich won his third straight point title at Mid-Continent in 1978. (Jerry Jacobs photo)

Jim Goettsche (14) challenges all-time Central Nebraska champ, Willie Hecke (Carrico 1), down the backstretch. (Jerry Jacobs photo)

Gene Scott's great looking coupe has a narrow lead over Todd Coker (4) and Frank Gates (9) at the Fairgrounds Speedway in Oklahoma City. The year was 1968. (Mar-Car photo)

Chapter 8
HOT CARS IN THE CITY
OKLAHOMA CITY, OKLAHOMA 1967-81

The State Fairgrounds at Oklahoma City became the promotional home of Bud Carson through his Mar-Car, Inc. Carson was one of the premier race directors in the country and OKC flourished as a supermodified haven during his reign.

In 1979, the racers themselves, in the name of the Oklahoma Racing Association, tried promoting the fairgrounds with little success. Car owner, Larry Hill took over in 1980, and brought the track back to Carson era popularity.

Lawton Speedway was another successful operation in the region, under the direction of Lanny Edwards. Jimmy Whitson (1970) and Roger Clark (1972) lost their lives while racing supers at the fairgrounds in Oklahoma City.

Oklahoma City 1967

Wiley veteran, Wayne Cox, was the champion at both Oklahoma City and Lawton in 1967-68. (Mar-Car photo)

OKC Nationals Champion, Harold Leep (LaVern Nance 11) noses to the inside of D. E. Suggs. (Mar-Car photo)

Carl Ferguson waves to the cameraman in his lowslung piece. (Mar-Car photo)

165

Evard Humphrey looks confident in his Larry Nailon sedan. This car featured four-wheel independent suspension. It must have worked because Humphrey won the 1967 Enid Speedway championship with it. (Mike Pogue collection)

Oklahoma City 1968

OKC veteran, Junior Garner seems pleased with his car. (Mar-Car photo)

Aaron Madden (1) shows Bobby Reynolds (Pat Suchy 33) and Bill Levesey the quick route through turn four. (Mar-Car photo)

Terry Linville had this beautiful sedan for the OKC competition. (Mar-Car photo)

Walter Barrett rolls up to the sign-in table with his "Singing 5" for driver, J. L. "Flash" Nash. (Jim Hysaw photo)

Oklahoma City 1969

Harold Leep (Ray Cates 2) chases down Bobby Reynolds. Leep was as close to unbeatable in 1969 as one man could be, winning the OKC, Tulsa and Wichita point titles. (Mar-Car photo)

A. J. Little won the first of three straight Lawton titles in 1969. (Mar-Car photo)

Tough Shady McWhorter came up from Dallas to win the Firecracker 100 at Lawton. (Mar-Car photo)

Second generation ace, Jackie Howerton (Del Torrance 1) rides the cushion around another super. (Mar-Car photo)

Oklahoma City 1970

Jackie Howerton (Jack Zink 1300) precedes Ron Brotherton (50) and Harold Leep (Cates 2). Howerton nailed down the OKC point title in 1970. (Mar-Car photo)

Melvin Rodgers (3), Emmett Hahn (Torrance 7) and Leep (Cates 2) all run the cushion. (Mar-Car photo)

Evard Humphrey with the immacualate Larry Nailon 12 was second to Jackie Howerton at OKC. (Mar-Car photo)

After Leep broke his leg in a mid-season mishap, Ron Fowler jumped aboard the Cates deuce. (Mar-Car photo)

The fairgrounds is getting crowded as Pat Patterson (106), Wallace Collins (40), Terry Linville (32), Jerry Holm (711) and Ron Brotherton (50) look for openings. (Mar-Car photo)

Oklahoma City 1971

Traffic Jam - Now, this is really crowded! Steve Foster (96), Bobby Reynolds (Suchy 33), Harold Leep (Cates 2), Emmett Hahn (Dr. Tom Garrett 55) and Benny Taylor (13) are among the identifiable. Leep won his second City title in '71. (Mar-Car photo)

Bill Bookout (50) and Mike Fleming (77) stay in line, as they scoot under another super at Oklahoma City. (Mar-Car photo)

Oklahoma City 1972

Larry Dewell (Bob Billups 112) and '72 Oklahoma City champ, Emmett Hahn (Garrett 55) duel. (Mar-Car photo)

Young Jim Harkness (Les Steinert 11) and vet, Evard Humphrey (Nailon 12), sail through turn four. (Mar-Car photo)

Melvin Rodgers retired after many fine seasons on the fairgrounds oval. (Mar-Car photo)

Steve Foster was a tough competitor at the Oklahoma State Fairgrounds. (Mar-Car photo)

Bobby Reynolds (Suchy 33) tries to break through the middle, while Emmett Hahn (Garrett 55) and Rodgers (3) hold steady. (Mar-Car photo)

Oklahoma City 1973

Joe Farley (91) and Bill Levesey (27) navigate around a spinning Scott Carson (10). Carson came back in a big way, winning two features plus the Oklahoma State Fair Championship at the end of the year. (Mar-Car photo)

Retired driver, Melvin Rodgers tapped young Bobby Walker to pilot his super. (Mar-Car photo)

Promoter Bud Carson seems happy that Jay Woodside has collected some of his fairgrounds loot. (Mar-Car photo)

Oklahoma City 1974

Benny Taylor teamed up with car owner, Pat Suchy, who produced this great looking machine. Taylor took it and produced an Oklahoma City point championship. (Tim Malone photo)

Dale Parson was a pretty good racer and he built some of the finest supers to grace a pit area. His wrap-around-T body style was a personel favorite of this writer. He, along with Jack Walker, Jelly Wilhelm and Verne Nance, provided most of the cars shown in the Tulsa, Wichita, OKC, Merrick and NCRA chapters of this book. (Tim Malone photo)

Larry Madden was having a strong season until his father, Aaron, was invovled in the Hutchinson, KS fire. (See page 192) (Mar-Car photo)

Bobby Walker continued to show that he was future championship material. (Mar-Car photo)

175

Oklahoma City 1975

Larry Holman won his second Oklahoma City point title in three years driving the Evert Walton 21. (Tim Malone photo)

Freddie Street's sharp looking Stafford & Franklin Special rests in the Lawton pits. (Mike Monatoboy photo)

Thad Dosher waits for the signal to fire up the Jerry Wilson 25 on OKC's frontstretch. (Tim Malone photo)

Oklahoma City 1976

Harold Leep prepares to dismount from his Suchy sled after another win at the fairgrounds. Harold won the City points for the third time in '76. (Mike Monatoboy photo)

Carl Wyatt's pride and joy sits in the pits before another Lawton adventure. James Skinner piloted it to the Lawton championship this year. (Mike Monatoboy photo)

Texan, Bob Ewell, started showing up at Lawton on a regular basis in '76 and impressed the railbirds with his hard charging style. (Mike Monatoboy photo)

Bobby Walker (James Plunkett 64) makes tracks through Oklahoma City's third bend on his way to challenging the veterans. (Mike Monatoboy photo)

177

Shane Carson shows off his good looking six-cylinder car before the start of the 1976 season. His crew sure does look excited! Shane's entrance into the supermodified arena made him the third of the Carson family at the fairgrounds. His father, Bud, promoted while his older brother, Scott, was a supermodified veteran by 1976. (Tim Malone photo)

Oklahoma City 1977

Simply put, Harold Leep was the best supermodified driver to ever come out of the plains states. Some may brag that they beat Leep here, or there, but no one beat Leep as often as Leep beat them. He won more championships at more tracks than anyone else featured in this book. In 1977, Leep took Pat Suchy's rig to a second straight Oklahoma City title the same way he won all the others, by being faster than most, and outlasting the rest. (Tim Malone photo)

Junior Bruner fought his way to the Lawton Speedway championship line in 1977. (Mike Monatoboy photo)

Larry Madden (1) looks to hold off a charging Ray Crawford (Harold Hillenburg 55) in Oklahoma City's fourth turn. (Sam Ewing photo)

Oklahoma City 1978

Bobby Walker (Plunkett 64) waits for hot laps to begin at Fairgrounds Speedway. The Walker and Plunkett team found all the pieces of the Oklahoma City puzzle in '78, winning the championship by the narrowest of margins over Harold Leep. Bobby's dad, Jack Walker, built some nice supers throughout the decade of the 1970's, including, of course, this one. (Mike Monatoboy photo)

Oklahoma City 1979

Darrell Jennings' right rear tire heads for the parking lot, as Darrell digs into the turn two guard rail. (Jeff Taylor photo)

Herb Lobdell (25) takes to the Armco banking in an effort to sneak around Ernest Jennings (61). He was less than successful with the pass. (Jeff Taylor photo)

181

Oklahoma City 1980

Darrell Jennings (81) has a half car length on Todd Coker (4), who has a wheel on Jim Lambert (92). Bobby Walker (16) takes the high side in an effort to close on all three. Walker took his second City and his first Lawton titles in 1980. (Jeff Taylor photo)

Paul Ott (0) has a slim lead over Ken Brewer (96) and Danny Shouse (27). (Jeff Taylor photo)

Emmett Hahn (left, John Davis 33) and Mike Peters (right, Larry Torson 1) dump themselves right in front of Howie Sewell. (Jeff Taylor photo)

Oklahoma City 1981

Missile Launch - Harold Leep (Lonnie Snowden 99) disputes Troy Matchen's (86) claim that the high groove is his. Leep won his fifth Oklahoma City title in 1981. (Jeff Taylor photo)

Rookie, Danny Wood (55), tries to hold off veteran, Darrell Jennings, on the Fairgrounds Speedway. Wood became World of Outlaws Rookie of the Year in 2000. (Jeff Taylor photo)

James Sheffield puts the pressure on "one-armed" Stan Constant (17). (Jeff Taylor photo)

Danny Shouse (Paul Shouse 27) applies the power as James Fessler (67) pushes his way through the corner at OKC. (Jeff Taylor photo)

Bob Peck (18) tries not to be a back seat driver while chasing Davey Moore (17) during the 1973 Hutchinson Nationals. Moore ran his six-cylinder car against the V-8's for several years, but didn't always have as much of a weight advantage as he did against Peck. (Jerry Leep photo)

Chapter 9
MARSHALL DILLON'S POSSE
THE MERRICK CIRCUIT of WESTERN KANSAS 1968-78

It was simply called "The Merrick Circuit." Jack Merrick merged the weekly shows at Dodge City (McCarty Speedway) with special events at the Kansas State Fairgrounds in Hutchinson and the Five State Fair in Liberal. Merrick also started his own version of "The Nationals" three years before Knoxville. After one year in Oklahoma City, he moved it to Hutchinson, where it still is today. The Hutchinson Nationals became one of the most prestigious and best paying events in the region playing to a full house more often than not.

At mid-season in 1977, Jack Merrick suffered a fatal heart attack at the age of 63. Even with his wife, Esther, continuing The Merrick Circuit through the 1978 season, an era of Western Kansas racing had come to an end.

There was also a Northwest Kansas tour, consisting of races at Wakeeny, Norton, Osborne and several other fairgrounds ovals.

No one was killed on The Merrick Circuit, during the supermodified era, but the 1974 Hutchinson Nationals crash and fire was one of the worst in supermodified history. The Northwest tour recorded one fatality, Ken Dierking, in 1972.

Frank Lies sits on Hutchinson's front straight in Kenny Riffle's sedan. Later on this same day, Lies won his third Hutch Nationals title. Behind Frankie, in the #52, is future Nationals winner, Jim Harkness, who finished 10th on this day. (Ken Greteman photo)

The Merrick Circuit 1968

Rocket 88 - Don Speier wheeled the sharp looking Paul Chance Olds 88 to The Merrick Circuit championship in 1968, then quit racing completely. (Ken Greteman photo)

Harold Leep poses with the gorgeous LaVern Nance built and owned super. (Ken Greteman photo)

D. E. Suggs (17) seems to be telling Harold Leep (Nance 999) that it's just some smoke and everything is OK. Leep isn't buying into it and prefers to wait on top of Hutchinson's wall for things to cool down. (Ken Greteman photo)

Terry Kowalsky (27) spins while Bill Bookout (50) gets a sudden push from Dick Hendershot (26). Emmett Hahn (Joe Cox 33) passes and wants no part of the highjinks. (Ken Greteman photo)

The Merrick Circuit 1969

Dale Reed prepares to qualify for the 1969 Hutchinson Nationals in Hap Looney's rig. (Ken Greteman photo)

Hutch' Nationals winner in 1966, Henry Ellington, doesn't look too happy about his prospects in 1969. (Ken Greteman photo)

Davey Ross has been a constant force to be reckoned with in his own 54. (Ken Greteman photo)

Jackie Howerton brought the Del Torrance Ace up from Tulsa, and set fast time at the Nationals. (Ken Greteman photo)

The Merrick Circuit 1970

Herb Copeland piloted Evart Isaac's hot rod to consecutive Merrick Circuit crowns in 1969 and 1970. His '69 run was particularly impressive, with the Kansas State Championship at Hutchinson, the Five State Fair title at Liberal, and a last lap win at the Hutch' Nationals. (Jerry Leep photo)

The Merrick Circuit 1971

Herb Copeland (Issac 8) works in front of the big crowd at Hutch', trying to stay ahead of Frankie Lies (Riffle 55). (Jerry Leep photo)

Dale Reed (Isaac 6) and Jim Harkness (Larry Prather 97) are staged and ready for another Western Kansas war. (Jerry Leep photo)

The Merrick Circuit 1972

A packed house looks on as pole sitter, Ron Fowler (John Schippert 4), and outside front row starter, Frank Lies (Prather 97) wait for the signal to fire up for the Hutchinson Nationals. Fowler led 48 of the 50 laps only to fall victim to a blown engine. Harold Leep won the event. (Jerry Leep photo)

Jerry Everhart prepares to climb aboard Buddy Cumley's "Triple Trey." (Jerry Leep photo)

Evard Humphrey (Larry Nailon 12) has his hands full trying to fend off the challenges of both Larry Dewell (Cumley 333) and Harold Leep (Ray Cates 2) at Hutchinson. (Ken Greteman photo)

The Merrick Circuit 1973

When Jim Harkness climbed into the Les Steinert ride for the '73 season, everyone else took a pay cut. Harkness ran the table on The Merrick Circuit, winning the Hutch Nationals, Kansas State Championship, Five State Championship and The Merrick Circuit point title. (Jerry Leep photo)

Davey Moore (17) tries to keep his six-cylinder ahead of Lee Martin's V-8. (Jerry Leep photo)

Herb Copeland (Isaac 8) is chased by Jerry Stone (Jerry Wilson 25) during action at Hutchinson. (Jerry Leep photo)

191

The Merrick Circuit 1974

THE HUTCHINSON FIRE

Mention the above words to any 1970's era supermodified fan and immediately he will take on a somber attitude. July 28, 1974, was the date of the Hutchinson Nationals, an event that fans and drivers alike considered the crown jewel of supermodified racing. A crowd of over 8000 jammed the Kansas State Fairgrounds for the traditional Sunday afternoon race. It was a typically hot and sunny July day, with the temperature over 100 degrees, as the 40-car field came down for the start of the championship 50-lapper. Even though the track had been repeatedly watered, the large field created a thick dust cloud that made it almost impossible for the back half of the field to see what was going on up front. At the end of the first lap, George Armstrong ran over the wheel of another car and flipped end-over-end several times. Almost instantly, other cars, blinded by the dust, started piling into each other with Aaron Madden's in the middle of the mess. His fuel tank exploded and the ensuing inferno engulfed the front straight. Madden, Jerry Soderberg and Jack Petty were badly burned with several other drivers receiving lesser injuries. Other drivers involved were Harold Lloyd Leep, Roy Bryant, Dutch ter Steege, D. E. Suggs, Johnny Boe, Buck Cadwell, Frank Lies and Fred Hembree. Hutchinson's fire fighting equipment proved woefully inadequate, and several race cars sat and burned to the ground before the Hutchinson City Fire Department arrived on the scene. It was a miracle that no one was killed in what was certainly one of the worst days in supermodified history. Jack Merrick and his crew bore considerable criticism in the months that followed, with quite a few fingers pointing at the track prep as one of the big factors. To his credit, Merrick was swift to take action, and the next year, a new water truck with a larger capacity was in use, as well as having a fire truck and full crew at the track. All three of the burned drivers returned to racing in one way or another. Madden was back in the Hutch' National field in 1975, Soderberg became a respected engine builder and Petty became a late model car owner.

The 1974 Hutchinson Nationals will forever be remembered for the frontstretch inferno that sent three drivers to the hospital with serious burns, totally destroyed several race cars and left several others badly damaged. (Jerry Leep photo)

Another view of the fire. D. E. Suggs' car, with the cockpit engulfed in flames, is in the foreground. Suggs was one of the fortunate drivers who escaped from their machines before the fire got to them. (Jerry Leep photo)

Dutch ter Steege watches helplessly as the burned out hulk that used to be his race car is pulled away from the crash scene. Note the expended fire extinguisher laying on the track just to the right of ter Steege. (Jerry Leep photo)

The Merrick Circuit 1975

The huge crowd notes as Roy Bryant (Harold Sparks 37) leads Jim Harkness (Steinert 11) down the front stretch at Hutchinson. This would prove to be the last summer for Harkness, as he was killed in a highway accident on February 28, 1976, not far from his Ness City, KS, home. He was 28 years old. (Jerry Leep photo)

Johnny Boe (Bill Baze 90) lifts the left front wheel while trying to keep Buck Cadwell (07) at bay during the Hutch' Nationals. (Mar-Car photo)

The Merrick Circuit 1976

Fred Hembree (79) dices with Duane Cain (58). Hembree won the first of his two Merrick titles in '76, with the other coming in 1978. (Jerry Leep photo)

Davey Moore (17) works the inside groove at Hutchinson on his way to the Kansas State Championship. Chasing him are Terry Uehling (Danny King 88) and Herb Copeland (Poor Boys Racing Team 15). (Jerry Leep photo)

Dave Frusher waves to the crowd before climbing into his Maurice Richardson 07. (Jerry Leep photo)

195

The Merrick Circuit 1977

Frank Lies (56) tangles with Bob Finley (20) in turn two at Hutch', while Eldon Borger (51) motors to the low side. (Warren Vincent photo)

Roger Thompson (Schippert 4) motors by Randy Jones (King 88) on the last lap of the B main at the Hutchinson Nationals. (Warren Vincent photo)

Duane Cain (58), Don Adams (1) and John Beeson (75) form a tight group in Hutchinson's third turn. (Warren Vincent photo)

The Merrick Circuit 1978

Legendary Jan Opperman (Wilson 25) pulls inside of Lee Martin (00) during the Hutch' Nationals. (Warren Vincent photo)

Dust Storm - Pete Elkins (G. W. Elkins 4) kicks up some dust with his low pass of Dee Zelmer (10). (Warren Vincent photo)

Gary Pletcher (06) makes an inside move on John Beeson (75) during the Kansas State Fair races. (Tim Hiatt photo)

Jon Johnson (86) needs to light a fire under his "Blue Flame Special" because Jan Opperman (Wilson 25) and Terry Uehling (Trade Winds 27) are ready to smoke by. (Jerry Leep photo)

Larry Coleman (Ray Riner 2) and Jay Woodside (Jelly Wilhelm 24) search for more speed at the Kansas State Fairgrounds oval, at Hutchinson, during the 1976 NCRA event. (Jerry Leep photo)

Chapter 10

LEAGUE OF CHAMPIONS
NATIONAL CHAMPIONSHIP RACING ASSOCIATION 1971-81

In February 1971, Bud Carson hosted a meeting of supermodified track promoters in the Kansas-Oklahoma-Texas region in hopes of putting together an organization that could standardize rules for all tracks. Thus, the NCRA was born. It was to be the first and only dirt track supermodified sanctioning body in the United States.

G. W. Elkins of Amarillo was the first president in 1971, followed by Carson (1972-73), Elkins again in 1974, and C. Ray Hall (1975-81).

Following the 1981 season, the NCRA changed the name of it's headlining division to dirt championship cars, and with that name change came the death knell to supermodified racing in the great southwest. In 1987 NCRA dropped the dirt champ cars in favor of sprint cars and is still going strong, with Hall still at the helm. NCRA's safety record for drivers was excellent, with not a single serious injury. However, Mike Conners was killed while flagging a NCRA race at Enid, OK, in 1974.

NCRA's first champion was Emmett Hahn of Tulsa. Hahn started the season in Del Torrance's car and won the first NCRA sanctioned race at Tulsa Speedway on May 30, 1971. When Jackie Howerton went USAC racing, Emmett took over the Jack Zink 1300, wrenched by Denny Moore. It was to be the beginning of a very successful 10-year run for the Hahn-Zink-Moore combo. (Mike Pogue collection)

NCRA 1971

Max Albright (91) and Jay Woodside (Bill Lewis 54) race searching for any advantage through turn two at Oklahoma City. (Mar-Car photo)

Grady Wade looks a bit pensive before climbing into his John Schippert mount for the Oklahoma City NCRA go. Grady needn't have worried, as he led all 50 laps of the A main to post an easy victory. (Mar-Car photo)

199

Garland Shepard (16) stands on the gas as Ray Crawford (Melvin Jarnagin 45) challenges at Tulsa. (Mike Pogue collection)

Grady Wade (John Schippert 4) and Jim Harkness (Larry Prather 97) battle for second place at Muskogee's 1971 NCRA round. Wade held off Harkness for the spot behind winner, Emmett Hahn. (Mike Pogue collection)

NCRA 1972

Joe Siefried (Gene Holoman 74), Larry Dewell (Bob Billups 112) and D. E. Suggs (11) try to hold off the charging duo of Emmett Hahn (Zink 01) and Harold Leep (Ray Cates 2). Leep and Hahn dominated the 1972 NCRA season with Hahn winning six races and Leep the other four. Leep won the championship. (Tim Malone photo)

Jerry Everhart (Pat Suchy 33) holds a slim lead over Melvin Rodgers (3) on Hutchinson's clay. Melvin posted a fourth place finish in the A feature this day, behind Harold Leep, Evard Humphrey and Emmett Hahn. (Tim Malone photo)

NCRA 1973

Harold Leep drove Aaron Madden's car to the 1973 NCRA championship even though he abruptly retired at the mid point of the season. Harold won at Lawton, Oklahoma City, Mesquite and Wichita before hanging up the goggles in late July. (Tim Malone photo)

George Armstrong wears the Paul Cunningham supermod after tangling with A. J. Little at Enid, OK. (Jerry Leep photo)

Roger Thompson (Schippert 04) is about to be set down a spot by Harold Leep (Madden 2) at Oklahoma City. Leep finished third behind George Armstrong and D. E. Suggs, with Thompson holding on for fourth. (Mar-Car photo)

NCRA 1974

Frankie Lies (56) leads Bob Brooks at the Devil's Bowl in Mesquite, TX. Lies won this race as well as Wichita Falls, TX and Lawton, OK, to secure his first NCRA title in 1974. Lies would go on to repeat in '75. (Mar-Car photo)

James McElreath (Jim McElreath 14) holds the inside line over George Armstrong (Melvin Horn 5) at Enid. (Jerry Leep photo)

Benny Taylor (Pat Suchy 13) and James McElreath (McElreath 14) ride the Devil's Bowl rim. McElreath had a great year in 1974, winning both the sprint and supermodified titles at the Devil's Bowl. (Mar-Car photo)

Jay Woodside (Leon Boomershine 77) slips inside of Ray Crawford (James Plunkett 64) in Tulsa action. (Tim Malone photo)

Frank Lies (56) charges around Johnny Suggs (Greig Lee 10) at the Devil's Bowl Speedway. Lies started 23rd in the field and won, going away, to record the NCRA feature win. (Mar-Car photo)

James McElreath pushes his Bill King Brake-O Special ahead of Ted Bacon at Tulsa. McElreath had a breakout season in '74, finishing just behind Frank Lies, in the NCRA standings. (Tim Malone photo)

This scene from turn four at Tulsa has Emmett Hahn (Zink 52) on the outside while Larry Holman (Evart Walton 21) and Ray Crawford (Plunkett 64) try to snatch the low groove. Holman ran consistently in NCRA with a third place points finish the result. (Tim Malone photo)

NCRA 1975

No. 1 vs. No. 1 - Texan, James McElreath (McElreath 1), battles Oklahoman, D. E. Suggs (Noel Crain 1), during a NCRA card at Tulsa Speedway. The McElreath car was originally built, by Jim, as a 96-inch wheelbase USAC dirt champ car and later converted to supermod specs for James. In mid-1975, they converted the car back to dirt champ specs and James made his USAC debut with it at Springfield, IL. Just when it looked like James could write his own ticket to stardom, he was killed in a USAC sprint race at Winchester, IN, in 1977. (Tim Malone photo)

Emmett Hahn (Zink 52) cruises in the black groove, while Randy Willingham (Jerry Wise 6) tries the slick outside at the Hutchinson Nationals. (Jerry Leep photo)

Ted Bacon (09) seems to be getting either a push start, or a wake up call from George Armstrong (Horn 5). Junior Taft (22) decides he wants no part of the shenanigans going on at Tulsa. (Tim Malone photo)

D. E. Suggs (Crain 1) has a slight lead over Jack Wickett (7) at Tulsa. Note the large right front tires on both cars! (Tim Malone photo)

NCRA 1976

Harold Leep (Pat Suchy 76) chases Emmett Hahn (Zink 52) and Ray Crawford (Harold Hillenberg 55) at Tulsa. Leep came out of retirement in late 1975, and joined forces with Suchy in '76 to secure his 3rd NCRA crown by winning events at Wichita Falls, Oklahoma City, Lawton, Wichita and Amarillo. (Tim Malone photo)

Randy Willingham (Wise 6) slides by Ted Bacon (9) at the Amarillo Speed Bowl in Texas. (Tim Malone photo)

Squeeze Play - Billy Brown (11x) goes into the spin cycle as Jon Johnson (Ray Charles & Johnson 86) tries to slip by. All this action took place at the Enid Winter Nationals. (Jerry Leep photo)

NCRA 1977

Jon Johnson (Johnson & Charles 86) battles with Eugene Hair (Tom Pace 7) at the Amarillo Speed Bowl. Hair is a four time Wichita Falls champion. (Warren Vincent photo)

Ray Crawford (Hillenberg 55) readies himself for the Tulsa feature. Alongside is Doran Raine (54) and the next row has Harold Lloyd Leep (Tim Malone photo)

Dale Reed (Isaac 6), Terry Uehling (Trade Winds 27) and Harold Lloyd Leep (2) charge into turn one at Hutchinson. (Tim Hiatt photo)

Terry Doss (Don Doss 96) duels with Odell Anderson at Tulsa. Doss picked up a big win at the Enid NCRA date, running away from Emmett Hahn, Ray Crawford and Jerry Stone. (Tim Malone photo)

Larry Holman (Tommy Sampson 21) didn't have a great year on the NCRA tour in 1977, but his consistency, through the years, lent itself well to the traveling circuit. He finished fifth in points in 1973, and third in '74. (Tim Malone photo)

NCRA 1978

Bob McCutchen (77) hangs on in anticipation of challenges from Ray Crawford (Hillenberg 55) and George Armstrong (Noel Crain & Danny Thurman 1) at Tulsa. Crawford logged his first NCRA championship in 1978, winning at Lawton, Enid and Tulsa. (Tim Malone photo)

Bob Cody (Wayne Dodson 43) uses his fat right front to stay in the black groove at Hutchinson. Cody's staunch support of NCRA was rewarded in 1978 with a fourth place finish in season points. Bob also won his fifth Amarillo Speed Bowl championship in 1978. (Warren Vincent photo)

Another long time supporter of NCRA from Amarillo is Randy Willingham. Although Randy had a sub-par year in '78, he had top ten point finishes in 1974 (8th) and 1977 (6th). (Jerry Leep photo)

210

George Armstrong had his beautiful Gary Stanton built unit humming along nicely on the NCRA trail for owners Noel Crain and Danny Thurman. The team netted a sixth in the final NCRA rundown, while picking off a win at Wichita Falls, TX. (Tim Malone photo)

NCRA 1979

The King and I - 1979 NCRA Champ, Dave Frusher (Danny King 88) duels with George Armstrong (Crain & Thurman 1) at Wichita. Frusher picked up wins at Amarillo and Enid during the season. (Jerry Leep photo)

Jerry Walkingstick (61) tries to hold to the spot Walt McWhorter (98) thinks is his. (Jerry Leep photo)

Terry Uehling (Don Carpenter 88) and Mark Walinder (78) glide over the 81 Speedway clay. Uehling gave Dave Frusher a run for his money, but came up just short of the NCRA crown. He won features at Lawton and Dewey, OK, in 1979. (Jerry Leep photo)

Former NCRA champs, Ray Crawford (Hillenberg 55) and Harold Leep (Lonnie Snowden 99) battle at the Hutchinson Nationals. Crawford won at the Devil's Bowl and Tulsa, while Leep spent the year working on "guidance" problems with his "missile." (Jerry Leep photo)

NCRA 1980

Jerry Stone piloted his Steve Carbone prepared OFIXCO Special of Lloyd K. Stephens to his first NCRA title in 1980 by winning at Muskogee and Amarillo. (Mike Monatoboy photo)

Harold Leep (Snowden 99) won his fourth Hutch Nationals and added two wins at Wichita and one at Enid in NCRA competition. (Mike Monatoboy photo)

Fred Hembree (79) and Dave Frusher (Larry Torson 1) slide through the dust at Oklahoma City with Harold Leep (Snowden 99) on their tails. (Jeff Taylor photo)

213

Bill Reynolds gets a flying start to the parking lot at Oklahoma City. Reynolds was not seriously injured during his airborne stunt, but the car's resale value suffered tremendously. (Jeff Taylor photo)

NCRA 1981

Herb Copeland stands on the gas in Carol Nance's latest creation. Herb won at Dallas, Muskogee, Oklahoma City and Lawton to claim his first, and NCRA's last, supermodified championship. Carol Nance is the son of famed car builer, LaVern Nance. (Mike Monatoboy photo)

Jerry Stone (Stephens 21) and Emmett Hahn (Zink 52) look for an advantage upon entering Oklahoma City's backstretch. (Jeff Taylor photo)

Troy Matchen (86) and Terry Coker (4) team up to hold off defending NCRA kingpin, Jerry Stone (Stephens 21) at Oklahoma City. (Jeff Taylor photo)

215

Car owner, Jack Moss and his driver, Lyndon Moss, wait for the signal to fire up their supermodified for the 1969 Southwestern Championships at Amarillo, Texas. (Leroy Byers photo)

Epilogue

So, what happened? The racing class that dominated short tracks in the 1960's had virtually disappeared by the end of the 1980's. Of course, supermodifieds are still around, but they are strictly a creature of the asphalt jungle now. In the last 20 years, a few tracks have tried to resurrect the dirt version of the super, with no success.

What happened was, in a word, conformity. It was in the decade of the 1970's that the short track race car factories began to take over. Led by Hall of Fame builders such as Bob Trostle and LaVern Nance, the most diversified form of auto racing that the world has ever seen, supermodifieds, were homogenized. It became easier for racers to buy cars and parts from a builder, knowing that if they break a part, the replacement is only a phone call away. Certainly easier and more efficient than rummaging through a junk yard, then going home and welding, grinding and hammering until the part fit. Since most sprint car clubs had rules and limits as to what a sprint car could look like, it was easier to build a car that resembled the traditional sprint car and race it as a super, than to build a super and then either sit in the stands, or try to convert it to sprint configuration, when the traveling clubs came to town.

Maybe though, that's not quite what happened. Maybe it's just the names that have changed. The builders built the cars; the racers bought the cars. That is true today just as it was in 1970. Supers started looking more and more like sprints; more and more people jumped on the name changing band wagon. Maybe that is all that has changed.

The fact is that the first race car to wear an overhead airfoil was a supermodified, and supers were beasts of the weekly racing wars. In the 1960's, supermodifieds were the most popular form of short track racing in the country. Winged sprints are certainly one of the most popular, if not the most popular, form of short track car today. In its original form, the Knoxville Nationals was the crown jewel of all weekly supermodified racing. Now it's the crown jewel of winged sprint car racing.

At the 2001 Eagle World of Outlaws Nationals, Sammy Swindell came out with some controversial body panels on his winged sprint. Denny Hegel, a friend of mine, upon viewing Swindell's car, stated in no uncertain terms, "That thing looks more like a supermodified than a sprint car!" Hey, you know what, maybe, the thing **IS A SUPERMODIFIED!**

The Dean Sylvester racing team prepares their supermodified for the 1961 Jayhawk Nationals. (Tom Powell photo)

Sammy Swindell gets on the loud pedal in his supermodified during the 2001 Eagle Nationals. (Bob Mays photo)

A Champion's Champion - Harold Leep ready to go to work in his office. This one happens to be the Pat Suchy Chevy with which he convincingly won the 1976 NCRA title. (Tim Malone photo)

Champions

Olympic Stadium
Kansas City, MO

	Driver	Car Owner
1955	Bill Chenault	Otto Haggert, 7
1956	Junior Hower	own, 24
1957	Junior Hower	own, 24
1958	Junior Hower	own, 24
1959	Junior Hower	own, 24
1960	Junior Hower	own, 24
1961	Jerry Weld	own, 93
1962	Junior Hower	own, 24
1963	Junior Hower	own, 24
1964	Ray Lee Goodwin	Duck Corum & Tom Purvis, 13
1965	Ray Lee Goodwin	own, 13
1966	Ray Lee Goodwin	Luther Brewer, 97
1967	Gene Gennetten	Bill Rhine, 300
1968	Gene Gennetten	Bill Rhine, 300
1969	Bob Williams	Jack Cunningham, 14
1970	Gene Gennetten	Bill Rhine, 85
1971	Gene Gennetten	own, 3
1972	Gene Gennetten	own, 3

Muskogee Speedway
Muskogee, OK

1967	Al Lemmons	Ray Cates, 2
1968	Buddy Cagle	Jack Zink, 52
1969	Jack Belk	Al Weiland, 37
1970	Chick Shaddox	own, 17

Riverside Stadium
North Kansas City, MO

	Driver	Car Owner
1955	Dave Allen	
1956	Jerry Weld	own, 93
1957	Jerry Weld	own, 93
1958	Bud Hunnicut	Bob Burns, 15
1959	Bud Hunnicut	Bob Burns, 15
1960	Virgil Chapman	own, 27
1961	Virgil Chapman	own, 27
1962	Bud Hunnicutt	Bill Underwood, 15
1963	Jerry Weld	own, 93
1964-67	?	
1968	Virgil Chapman	Dick Howard, 27

Mid-America Fairgrounds
Topeka, KS

1961	Bill Corwin	Jack Corwin, 4
1962	Don Elliott	Roy Still, 1
1963	Don Elliott	Roy Still, 1
1964	Don Elliott	Roy Still, 1
1965	Ken Williams	Roy Still, 1
1966	Ray Lee Goodwin	Luther Brewer, 97
1967	Ray Lee Goodwin	Luther Brewer, 97
1968	Dick Sutcliffe	Gary Hanna, 29
	& Thad Dosher	own, 74
1969	Bob Williams	Jack Cunningham, 14
1970	Thad Dosher	Gary Hanna, 14
1971	Ray Lee Goodwin	C. Williams & G. Swenson, 24
1972	Jay Woodside	Gary Moulin, 1

Marion County Fairgrounds
Knoxville, IA

	Driver	Car Owner
1958	Earl Wagner	Slim Gutnecht, 77
1959	Earl Wagner	Slim Gutnecht, 77
1960	Jerry Hayes	Still & Hanna, 11
1961	Earl Wagner	Dean Sylvester, 12
1962	Bud McCune	own, 103
1963	Greg Weld	own, 92
1964	Bill Utz	own, 98
1965	Jerry Blundy	own, 33
1966	Jerry Blundy	own, 33
1967	Bill Utz	Bill Gault, 98
1968	Dick Sutcliffe	Gary Hanna, 29
1969	Bob Williams	Jack Cuningham, 14
1970	Joe Saldana	B. Chadborne & J. Leverenz, 2
1971	Ray Lee Goodwin	C. Williams & G. Swenson, 24
1972	Lonnie Jensen	Larry Swanson, 14

Nebraska Modified Racing Association
Eagle Raceway   **Midwest Speedway**
Eagle, NE   **Lincoln, NE**

1964	Lloyd Beckman	Bill Smith, 4x
1965	John Wilkinson	C. Williams & G. Swenson, 24
1966	Lloyd Beckman	C. Williams & G. Swenson, 24
1967	Larry Upton	Ed Smith, 44
1968	Lloyd Beckman	Larry Swanson, 14
1969	Lloyd Beckman	Larry Swanson, 14
1970	Ray Lee Goodwin	C. Williams & G. Swenson, 24
1971	Lloyd Beckman	Bill Smith, 4x
1972	Lonnie Jensen	Larry Swanson, 14
1973	Lonnie Jensen	Ed Smith, 44
1974	Dick Sutcliffe	Dave Van Patten, 18

81 Speedway
Wichita, KS

	Driver	Car Owner
1965	Harold Leep	Warren Wilhelm, 99
1966	Harold Leep	Warren Wilhelm, 99
1967	Harold Leep	Warren Wilhelm, 99
1968	Walt McWhorter	own, 98
1969	Harold Leep	Ray Cates, 2
1970	Frank Lies	Kenny Riffle, 55
1971	Dale Reed	Evart Isaac, 6
1972	Dale Reed	Evart Isaac, 6
1973	Dale Reed	Evart Isaac, 6
1974	—	
1975	Roy Bryant	Harold Sparks, 37
1976	Walt McWhorter	own, 98
1977	Walt McWhorter	own, 98
1978	Walt McWhorter	own, 98
1979	Dale Reed	Jerry Wilson, 25
1980	Walt McWhorter	own, 98

Dewey Speedway
Dewey, OK

1974	Ted Bacon	own, 09
1975	Ted Bacon	own, 09
1976	Mike Peters	Norman Gum, 71
1977	Mike Peters	Norman Gum, 71
1978	Court Grandstaff	own, 9

Oklahoma Fair Speedway
Oklahoma City, OK

	Driver	*Car Owner*
1967	Wayne Cox	own, 161
1968	Wayne Cox	own, 161
1969	Harold Leep	Ray Cates, 2
1970	Jackie Howerton	Jack Zink, 1300
1971	Harold Leep	Ray Cates, 2
1972	Emmett Hahn	Dr. Tom Garrett, 55
1973	Larry Holman	own, 21
1974	Benny Taylor	Pat Suchy, 13
1975	Larry Holman	Evart Walton, 21
1976	Harold Leep	Pat Suchy, 76
1977	Harold Leep	Pat Suchy, 76
1978	Bobby Walker	James Plunkett, 64
1979	Mike Peters	Larry Hill, 10
1980	Bobby Walker	James Plunkett, 64
1981	Harold Leep	Lonnie Snowden, 99

Hastings Raceway
Hastings, NE

1967	Willie Hecke	John Davisson, 1
1968	Willie Hecke	John Davisson, 1
1969	Willie Hecke	John Davisson, 1
1970	Willie Hecke	John Davisson, 1
1971	Dean Ward	Mel Earnest & Don Wilson, 33
1972	Willie Hecke	Howard Carrico, 1
1973	Ron Williams	Ron Williams & Jim Ellett, 29
1974	Willie Hecke	Howard Carrico, 1

Lawton Speedway
Lawton, OK

	Driver	*Car Owner*
1967	Wayne Cox	own, 161
1968	Wayne Cox	own, 161
1969	A. J. Little	C. H. Malone, 24
1970	A. J. Little	C. H. Malone, 24
1971	A. J. Little	own, 10
1972	J. L. Nash	Clinton Herring, 5
1973	Jerry Douglas	Clyde Douglas, 43
1974	Eugene Hair	Ron Guiffery & Cope Miller, 4
1975	Eugene Hair	Ron Guiffery & Cope Miller, 12
1976	James Skinner	Carl Wyatt, 65
1977	Junior Bruner	own, 32
1978	Freddy Street	J. W. Boren, 55
1979	A. J. Little	own, 10
1980	Bobby Walker	James Plunkett, 64

Enid Speedway
Enid, Oklahoma

1967	Evard Humphrey	Larry Nailon, 12
1968	Bill Bookout	own, 50
1969	Ron Brotherton	own, 50
1970	Ron Brotherton	own, 50
1971	Bill Bookout	own, 50
1972	Larry Holman	own, 21

Tulsa Speedway
Tulsa, OK

	Driver	*Car Owner*
1966	Ron Fowler	Al Weiland, 37
1967	Buddy Cagle	Jack Zink, 52
1968	Buddy Cagle	Jack Zink, 52
1969	Harold Leep	Ray Cates, 2
1970	Jackie Howerton	Jack Zink, 1300
1971	Chick Shaddox	own, 17
1972	Emmett Hahn	Jack Zink, 01
1973	Emmett Hahn	Jack Zink, 52
1974	Derrill Brazeal	Junior Taft, 21
1975	Emmett Hahn	Jack Zink, 52
1976	Ray Crawford	Harold Hillenburg, 55
1977	Emmett Hahn	Jack Zink, 52
1978	Emmett Hahn	Jack Zink, 52
1979	George Armstrong	Noel Crain & Danny Thurman, 1
1980	Ray Crawford	Harold Hillenburg, 55
1981	Ray Crawford	Harold Hilenburg, 55
1982	Jerry Stone	Lloyd K. Stephens, 21
1983	Donnie Crawford	Harold Hillenburg, 56

Riveria Raceway
Norfolk, NE

1970	Jerry Suhr	own, 56
1971	Jerry Suhr	own, 56
1972	Don Weyhrich	own, $1.98
1973	Jerry Suhr	own, 56
1974	Gerald Bruggeman	own, 00
1975	Don Weyhrich	own, $1.98
1976	Don Weyhrich	own, $1.98

Mid-Continent Raceway
Doniphan, NE

	Driver	*Car Owner*
1972	Jim Goettsche	Ken Gappa & Jim Geottsche, 17
1973	Dean Ward	Mel Earnest & Don Wilson, 33
1974	Ron Williams	own, 29
1975	Ken McCarty	Mel Earnest, 11
1976	Don Weyhrich	own, $1.98
1977	Don Weyhrich	own, $1.98
1978	Don Weyhrich	own, $1.98

National Championship Racing Association

1971	Emmett Hahn	Jack Zink, 52
1972	Harold Leep	Ray Cates, 2
1973	Harold Leep	Aaron Madden, 2
1974	Frank Lies	own, 56
1975	Frank Lies	own, 56
1976	Harold Leep	Pat Suchy, 76
1977	Emmett Hahn	Jack Zink, 52
1978	Ray Crawford	Harold Hillenburg, 55
1979	Dave Frusher	Danny King, 88
1980	Jerry Stone	Lloyd K. Stephens, 21
1981	Herb Copeland	Carol Nance, 1n

Skylark Speedway
Columbus, NE

	Driver	*Owner*
1967	Willie Hecke	John Davisson, 1
1968	Willie Hecke	John Davisson, 1
1969	—	
1970	Jim Stewart	Fred Garbers, 69
1971	Gerald Bruggeman	R. D. Bisping, 00

The Merrick Circuit
McCarty Speedway   Kansas State Fairgrounds
Dodge City, KS   Hutchinson, KS

Five State Fair
Liberal, KS

1968	Don Spreier	Paul Chance, 88
1969	Herb Copeland	Evart Isaac, 8
1970	Herb Copeland	Evart Isaac, 8
1971	Dale Reed	Evart Isaac, 6
1972	Dale Reed	Evart Isaac, 6
1973	Jim Harkness	Les Steinert, 11
1974	Herb Copeland	Evart Issac, 8
1975	Dale Reed	Evart Issac, 6
1976	Fred Hembree	own, 79
1977	Terry Uehling	Trade Winds, 27
1978	Fred Hembree	own, 79

Gage County Fairgrounds
Beatrice, NE

	Driver	*Car Owner*
1967	Freeman Hudson	own, 54
1968	Ken Parde	own, 95
1969	Wayne Holz	own, 73
1970	Lonnie Jensen	Larry Swanson, 14
1971	Lloyd Beckman	Bill Smith, 4x

Kearney Raceway
Kearney, NE

1967	Willie Hecke	John Davisson, 1
1968	Willie Hecke	John Davisson, 1
1969	Willie Hecke	John Davisson, 1
1970	Willie Hecke	Bob Strong, 1
1971	Willie Hecke	Bob Strong, 1

1966 Tulsa champ, Ron Fowler (John Schippert 4x), 1979 Tulsa champ, George Armstrong (Paul Cunningham 8) and 1973 Lawton champ, Jerry Douglas (Clyde Douglas 43) look for escape routes from an Enid skirmish in 1973. (Jerry Leep photo)

Index

Abbott, Roger, 148
Ackerman, Lee, 10
Adams, Don, 196
Adler, Jim, 152, 157-158
Agan, Craig, 9
Albright, Max, 199
Aldrich, Charlie, 35
Aldrich, Red, 152, 156
Allen, Dave, 219
Anderson, Odell, 88, 208
Andrews, Red, 47
Anno, Bill, 43, 46
Argabright, Dave, 10
Armstrong, George, 97, 104, 192, 202-203, 206, 210-212, 222-223
Ash, Lou, 9
Atkins, Jerry "Flea," 58
Austin, Sam, 77

Babb, John, 60, 67, 70, 76
Backlund, Jon, 9, 25-27, 35, 39, 80, 138
Bacon, Ted, 204, 206-207, 220
Bahr, Butch, 10, 143
Baker, Ken, 28
Barclay, Tom, 9
Barker, Keith, 10, 31, 35-36, 38-39, 58
Baldus, Al, 23, 73
Barnett, Gene, 10
Barnett, Glenna, 10
Barnett, Walter, 167
Bauerfind, Barney, 29
Baze, Bill, 194
Beckman, Lloyd, 7, 10, 66, 71, 125-126, 128, 131, 138-139, 220, 223
Beeson, John, 196-197
Belk, Jack, 41, 46-47, 51, 84, 90, 219
Bell, Jerry, 10, 150

Bender, Duane, 10, 148, 151, 153
Berry, Claude, 46
Billups, Bob, 172, 201
Biskup, Jerry, 125, 130
Bisping, R. D., 141, 155, 223
Blackett, Ralph, 10, 135, 142
Blazek, Bob, 10
Blundy, Jerry, 58, 69-71, 74, 79, 82, 220
Boe, Johnny, 192, 194
Bogue, George & Melton, Don, 130, 132
Bookout, Bill, 171, 186, 221
Boomershine, Leon, 203
Booth, Joe, 38
Bond, James, 52, 73
Boren, J. W., 221
Borger, Eldon, 196
Borofsky, Stan, 25, 137
Boskens, Pete, 80
Bowes, Ed, 10, 127, 132-133
Brahmer, Rich, 130
Brahmer, Russ, 12, 130, 149
Brazeal, Derrill, 92, 96, 98, 100, 103, 222
Brennfoerder, Frank, 7, 10, 124, 128, 134, 156, 158
Brennfoerder, Frank & Starr, Duane, 124
Brewer, Brenda, 28
Brewer, Ken, 182
Brewer, Luther, 9, 27-28, 36, 41, 51-52, 54, 57, 71, 219
Brinkman, Woody, 10
Brooks, Bob, 203
Brotherton, Ron 169-170, 221
Brown, Allan, 10
Brown, Billy, 207
Brown, Don, 38
Brown, Emmerson, Rutherford & Layne, 91
Brown, Terry, 117
Brudigan, Gene, 158-159, 163
Brudigan, Harold, 160
Bruggeman, Gerald "Boog," 10, 155, 159, 162, 222-223
Bruner, Junior, 179, 221

Bryant, Roy, 10, 110, 116-117, 192, 194, 220
Bryson, Ruth, 19
Buettenbach, Dutch, 139
Burdick, Bob, 10, 47
Burke, Al, 28
Burling, Dean, 130
Burns, Bob, 18-20, 51, 219
Burns, Doug, 25
Butcher, Mike, 10
Bybee, Darrell, 120
Byers, Leroy, 10

Cadwell, Buck, 192, 194
Cagle, Buddy, 10, 86-88, 91, 93, 219, 222
Cahill Brothers, 82
Cain, Duane, 195-196
Capps, Jim, 88
Carbone, Steve, 213
Carey, Roy, 29
Carico, Howard, 157, 161, 221
Carl's Hollywood Muffler Shop Special, 16
Carlson, Don, 75
Carpenter, Don, 212
Carson, Bud, 9, 13, 165, 174, 178, 199
Carson, Scott, 174, 178
Carson, Shane, 9-10, 178
Carver, Sparky, 29-31, 36
Casper, Billy Jack, 110
Cates, Ray, 89, 90, 112, 168-171, 190, 201, 219-222
Cattrell, Wylan, 117, 120
Chadborne, Bill, & Leverenz, John, 77, 134, 220
Chance, Paul, 185, 223
Chapman, Virgil, 20, 219
Charles, Ray & Johnson, Jon, 122, 207-208
Chenault, Bill, 15, 219
Christenson, Roger, 52
Christian, K. O., 113
Clark, George, 52
Clark, Ron, 165
Cody, Bob, 210
Cohee, Bill, 43, 48-49, 71

Coker, Terry, 215
Coker, Todd, 164, 182
Coleman, Forest, 113
Coleman, Larry, 198
Collins, Wallace, 170
Colvin, Terry, 102
Conners, Mike, 199
Constant, Stan, 183
Cooper, Don, 29
Cooper, J. L., 21, 36, 39, 78
Copeland, Herb, 113, 115, 118, 188-189, 191, 195, 215, 222-223
Corbin, Tom, 31, 58
Corum, Duck & Purvis, Tom, 24, 49, 219
Corwin, Bill, 42, 44, 219
Corwin, Jack, 42, 44, 219
Covert, Bill, 44
Covert, Oren, 56
Cox, "Iron Head," 16
Cox, Joe, 90, 95, 186
Cox, Wayne, 165, 221
Craig, Bruce, 10
Craig, Don, 59
Crain, Noel, 205-206
Crain, Noel & Thurman, Danny, 104, 210-212, 222
Crawford, Donnie, 105, 222
Crawford, Ray, 13, 96, 100-101, 179, 200, 203-204, 207-208, 210, 212, 222
Crear, Mark, 129
Crouch, Bill, 87
Crook, Kenny, 65
Cumley, Buddy, 190
Cummings, Wendell, 147
Cunningham, Jack, 33, 35-37, 54, 56-57, 72, 76, 219-220
Cunningham, Paul, 97, 202, 223
Curless, Bill, 111
Curless, Carl, 111
Curtis, Bill, 28, 73

Dake, Wayne, 10

Davis, Cecil, 17
Davis, John, 182
Davisson, John, 144, 150-151, 221, 223
Daniels, Gene, 85
DeCarlo, Al, 62
Delano, Jack, 61
DeVolder, Tom, 19
Dewell, Larry, 11, 115. 172, 190, 201
Diaz, Dan, 87
Dickenson, Marv, 151
DiCorce, Ernie, 137
Dierking, Ken, 185
Dillard, Bill, 85
Dishinger, Art, 47-48
Dix, John, 36
Dodson, Wayne, 210
Doiel, Cliff "Grandstand," 153-154
Dole, M. E., 137
Dosher, Thad, 44, 49, 57, 68, 72, 83, 140, 176, 219
Doss, Don, 208
Doss, Terry, 208
Douglas, Clyde, 221, 223
Douglas, Jerry, 221, 223
Droud, Don, 127, 141
Droz, Froggy, 66
Dunkle, Gary, 142
Durrett, Stan, 85
Dutton, Paul, 112
Duvall, Junior, 88

Earnest, Mel & Wilson, Don, 221-222
Earnest, Mel, 158, 160, 222
Edeal, George, 9
Edmunds, Don, 13
Edwards, Lanny, 165
Egan, Tom, 148
Elkins, G. W., 197, 199
Elkins, Pete, 197
Ellington, Henry, 187
Elliott, Don, 46-47, 219
Ellis, Leroy, 85

Eubanks, James, 95
Evans, Jack, 152-153
Everhart, Jerry, 11, 118, 201
Ewell, Bob, 105, 177

Fallsted, Buck, 7
Fann, Bill, 152, 156-157
Farley, Joe, 174
Farmer, Al "Cotton," 107
Felker, Corky, 91
Ferguson, Carl, 165
Ferrand, Wes, 22, 48, 51
Fernyhough, Scott, 11
Fessler, James, 183
Fetger, Ron, 155
Finley, Bob, 196
Finnery, Hugh, 85
Fitzgerald, Ed, 29
Flanagan, Ray, 160
Fleming, Mike, 171
Forbes, Ralph, 11
Ford, Bob, 29
Forshee, Jeff, 121, 123
Forshee, Pete, 121, 123
Forshee, Red, 110
Foster, Steve, 171, 173
Fowler, Ron, 86, 170, 190, 221, 223
Foyt, A. J., 136
Friendly Chevrolet, 109
Fries, Dick, 51
Frusher, Dave, 195, 212-213, 222
Furr, Don, 30

Gappa, Ken & Goettsche, Jim, 156, 158, 222
Garbers, Fred, 148, 151, 162, 223
Garner, Bob, 107, 109
Garner, Junior, 167
Garrett, Dr. Tom, 171-173, 221
Gates, Frank, 164
Gault, Bill, 72, 220
Gearhart, Ace, 120
Gennetten, Gene, 10, 30, 37, 39, 54, 58, 131, 219

225

Gerdes, Jerry, 125, 130
Gessford, Jim, 11
Gibson, Jack, 23
Gibson, Marvin, 34
Gilbert, Jerry, 21, 23, 45, 65
Gilespy, Gary, 152
Gillen, Ray, 155, 157
Glenn, Tony, 10
Goettsche, Jim, 11, 156, 158, 163, 222
Golden, Jim, 140, 142
Goodrich, Fred, 129
Goodrich, Ray, 58
Goodwin, Ray Lee, 24, 25, 27-28, 36, 48-49, 52-54, 57-59, 71, 74, 82, 133, 135, 219-220
Gordon, Jimmy, 154
Gosnell, Larry, 155
Grabill, Lynn, 11, 148, 156-157, 159
Granatelli, Andy, 61
Grandstaff, Court, 120, 220
Graves, Harry, 58
Grein, Louis, 153, 154
Greteman, Ken, 9
Gritz, Kenny, 76, 124, 126
Guiffery, Ron & Miller, Cope, 221
Gumm, Norman, 116, 119, 220
Gunter Signs Special, 110
Guttnecht, Slim, 62, 66, 220

Haack, Doug, 11
Haack, Stan, 11, 12, 152-153
Haase, Bob, 161
Haase, Ray, 147, 161, 162
Haberer, Mike, 159, 161
Haggert, Otto, 15, 219
Hahn, Emmett, 11, 90, 92-93, 96-97, 100, 103, 169, 171-173, 182, 186, 199-201, 204, 206-208, 215, 221-222
Hair, Eugene, 208, 221
Hall, Bill, 107
Hall, C. Ray, 107, 199
Hall, Ted, 71, 110
Halteman, Ken, 58

Hamby, Chet, 41
Hampton, Shot, 117
Hanna, Gary, 37, 46, 49, 53, 55-57, 71, 74-75, 140, 219-220
Harkness, Jim, 115, 172, 185, 189, 191, 194, 200, 223
Harmon, Whitey, 38
Harrington, Paul, 102
Harrison, Bill, 41, 52
Hatch, Bud, 90
Hayes, Jerry, 41, 46, 52, 68, 219
Harper, Ken, 19, 24, 69
Hecke, Willie, 126, 130, 145, 150-152, 155, 157, 161, 163, 221, 223
Heckman, Herb, 139, 141
Heble, Jim, 132, 138
Hegel, Dennis, 11, 217
Helms, Sonny, 61, 63-64
Hembree, Fred, 119, 192, 195, 213, 223
Hendershot, Dick, 186
Herring, Clinton, 221
Hiatt, Tim, 11
Hibbard, Roy, 30, 32, 35-36, 38, 71
Hibbard, Russ, 29-31, 36, 58
Hibbs, George, 55
Hightshoe, Keith, 54, 128, 137, 140
Hill, Bill, 11
Hill, Larry, 165, 221
Hill, Ruby, 10
Hillenberg, Harold, 101, 105, 179, 207-208, 210, 212, 222
Hite, George, 132, 138
Hoffman, Charles, 11
Hollamon, Guy, 125, 132
Hollifield, Ben, 76
Holliman, Dan, 134, 138, 140
Holliman, Stan, 130, 134, 138, 140
Hollingsworth, Larry, 61
Holm, Jerry, 170
Holman, Fred, 29
Holman, Larry, 176, 204, 209, 221
Holmes, Jerry, 11, 159, 161

Holoman, Gene, 97, 201
Holz, Wayne, 130, 223
Hoover, Ken, 144
Hoppenstedt, Francis, 111
Horn, Melvin, 203, 206
Horner, Arnold, 107
Howard, Dick, 28, 55, 73, 219
Hower, Junior, 17-20, 49, 219
Howerton, Angelo, 92
Howerton, Jackie, 90-92, 168-169, 187, 199, 221-222
Hudson, Freeman, 223
Humphrey, Evard, 89, 166, 170, 172, 190, 201, 221
Hunnicutt, Bud, 9, 11, 15, 17-20, 23, 219
Hurley, Bob, 119

Irwin, Don, 41
Isaac, Evart, 113, 115-116, 118-119, 188-189, 191, 208, 220, 223

Jacobs, Jerry, 10
Janssen, Jerry "Yogi," 134
Jarnigan, Melvin, 95, 200
Jefferies, Claude, 46
Jennings, Darrell, 181-183
Jennings, Ernest, 13, 181
Jensen, Lonnie, 73, 83, 129, 133-135, 139, 141-142, 220, 223
Jimerson, Mike, 92, 94
Johnson, Doug, 92, 96
Johnson, Jon, 122, 197, 207-208
Jolly, Dave, 146
Jones, Randy, 196
Jordan, Rex, 7, 130

Kallweit, Leroy, 130, 149
Kelly Pontiac Special, 34
Kelly, Vince, 137
Kettleson, Rod, 47
Kidwell, Chuck, 155

King, Bill "Brake-O", 204
King, Danny, 195-196, 212, 222
King, Grant, 59
King, Sonny, 49
Kissenger, Don, 152
Kowalsky, Terry, 186
Kneisler, Ken, 41
Knoedler, Rod, 139
Kraft, Charlie, 9, 16-17, 21-22, 25
Kropp, Harvey, 125
Krueger, Armin, 11
Krueger, Dan, 61, 73
Kunzman, Lee, 75

Lahodny, Leon, 128, 130, 132
Lamb, Doc, 111
Lambert, Jim, 182
Lambert, Tom, 93
Lammers, Mel, 152, 156, 159, 161
Lane, Roger, 59, 71
Larson, Jud, 23
Larson, Roger, 78, 140
Laster, Tom, 88
Lawrence, Bob, 11
Layne, Jack, 95
Leavitt, Ed, 13, 14, 28, 38-39, 55, 58, 82, 140-141
Lee, Grieg, 204
Leep, Harold, 10, 11, 90, 106-107, 110, 112, 116, 120, 123, 131, 165, 168-171, 177, 179, 183, 185-186, 190, 201-202, 207, 212-213, 218, 220-222
Leep, Harold Lloyd, 11, 192, 208
Leep, Jerry, 9
Leighty, Jim, 14
Lemmons, Al, 89, 98, 219
Levesey, Bill, 167, 174
Lewis, Bill, 93, 199
Liekam, Pete, 125
Lies, Frank, 55, 110, 113, 116, 185, 189-190, 192, 196, 203-204, 220, 222
Lilly, Cliff, 17, 27

Lingenfelter, Kim, 162
Linville, Terry, 167, 170
Little, A. J., 168, 202, 221
Lobdell, Herb, 181
Logan, Larry, 41
Long Chevy, 39, 78
Looney, Hap, 187
Looper, Dale, 123
Lucas, Gordon, 117
Luginbill, Wayne, 126-127
Lyle, Jay, 73
Lynch, Chuck, 36

Macklin, Homer, 150, 153
Madden, Aaron, 100, 167, 175, 192, 202, 222
Madden, Larry, 100, 175, 179
Mahoney, Jim, 78, 138
Malone, C. H., 221
Malone, Tim, 9
Manning, Al, 25
Marsh, Buddy, 42, 52
Martin, Lee, 191, 197
Mascaro, Angelo, 66
Matchen, Troy, 183, 215
Maurer, Don, 146, 151, 157
Maxwell, Don, 141
McCain, Roy, 125, 132
McCarty, Dale, 58, 78
McCarty, Ken, 156-157, 160, 222
McChesney, Don, 11
McClelland, Mike, 102
McCune, Bud, 65, 220
McCutchen, Bob, 116, 210
McDaniels, Dale, 19, 91
McElreath, James, 203-205
McElreath, Jim, 203, 205
McFarland, Jud, 17
McGee, Mike, 99
McGee, Phil, 99
McMurrary, Jim, 24
McVay, Ed, 36

McWhorter, Shady, 168
McWhorter, Walt, 107, 111, 113, 115, 119, 212, 220
Merrick, Ester, 185
Merrick, Jack, 185, 192
Mickelson, Ray, 152, 158
Milbourn, Dave, 130, 146, 148
Miller Chevy, 32, 35-36, 38
Miller, Ron & Moon, Gay, 150
Miller, Ted, 156, 157
Moffett, Mel, 58, 74-75, 79, 82
Moore, Bob, 80
Moore, Bobby, 11
Moore, Dale, 28, 30, 73
Moore, Dave, 123, 184, 191, 195
Moore, Denny, 86-87, 199
Morosic, Lonnie, 132, 138, 160
Moss, Lyndon, 216
Moss, Jack, 216
Moulin, Gary, 59, 219
Moyer, Bill, 63, 71, 74
Mullen, Pinky, 111
Murie, "Big Al," 11, 22, 110, 136
Murie, Rick, 39
Murie, Tom, 22
Myers, Ken, 112
Myles Engineering, 81

Nailon, Larry, 89, 166, 170, 172, 190, 221
Nance, Carol, 215, 222
Nance, LaVern, 108, 165, 175, 185-186, 215, 217
Nash, J. L. "Flash," 167, 221
Nehr, Don, 88
Nelson, Bill, 107, 109
Nichols, Bill, 118
Nickolite, Bob, 10
North, Larry, 107
Norris, Jack, 80
Nun, Rex, 142

Offutt, Frank, 109
Oltman, Denny, 11, 129, 137

O'Neil, Bob, 144, 155, 157
Opperman, Jay, 61
Opperman, Jan, 76, 82, 133-134, 197
Orth, Joe, 10
Ott, Paul, 182

Pace, Tom, 208
Paddock, Vic, 96
Parde, Ken, 80, 223
Parkinson, Ralph Jr., 9, 30, 134
Parkinson, Ralph, Sr., 9, 30, 60, 77
Parson, Dale, 175
Patterson, Larry, 11
Patterson, Pat, 88, 171
Peck, Bob, 184
Penney, Jim, 9
Penrod, Larry, 147-148, 150, 152
Perkins, Ron, 58
Perlich, Leonard, 85
Perry, Melvin, 158-159
Perry, Wendell, 158-159
Peters, Mike, 116, 119, 182, 220-221
Peterson, Merlin, 141
Peterson, Pete, 152
Petty, Jack, 192
Pletcher, Gary, 197
Plunkett, James, 96, 100, 177, 180, 203-204, 221
Pogue, Mike, 9
Pontious, George, 156-157
Poor Boys Racing Team, 118, 195
Powell, Tom, 10
Prather, Larry, 189-190, 200
Pugh, Bill, 65

Quattrocchi, Louie, 134

R & H Farms, 38, 58-59, 78, 83
Rager, Roger, 130, 133
Rain, Doran, 208
Ready, Ted, 65, 68
Reece, Phil, 73

Reed, Dale, 11, 54, 115-116, 119, 120, 122, 187, 189, 208, 220, 223
Reidy, Doug, 156, 161
Reynolds, Bobby, 167-168, 171, 173
Reynolds, Bill, 214
Rhine, Bill, 25, 30, 37, 54, 71, 131, 219
Rhoten, Eldon, Golden, Jim & Kelly, Vince, 137, 140, 142
Rice, Jeff, 47, 83
Richardson, Danny, 62, 63
Richardson, Jim, 9
Richardson, Maurice, 195
Richert, Jerry, 65, 68, 79
Riffle, Kenny, 55, 113, 185, 189, 220
Riggins, Jim, 11, 132, 140
Rigsby, Bill, 55
Riner, Ray, 108, 198
Riner, Rick, 123
Ring, Larry, 98
Roberts Bill, 36
Robbins, Roy, 64
Robinson, Marion, 61, 69, 72, 74
Rodgers, Melvin, 169, 173-174, 201
Roper, Dean, 91
Rosenberg, Ron, 51
Ross, Dave, 114, 187
Rosso, Bob, Alexander, Ron & Phillips, Mike, 156, 158
Rothgeb, Doug, 23
Roucha, Lyle, 147, 149
Royal, Ray, 78, 126, 132-133
Rudder, Arnie, 140
Rumsey, Dale, 134, 143
Rutland, Wayne, 126
Ryson Special, 105

Saldana, Joe, 11, 35, 72, 77, 134, 138, 220
Salem, Rick, 106
Sampson, Tommy, 209
Sanders, Bill, 90
Scanlon, Bob, 129

Schmeh, Tom, 9
Schonefeld, Don, 12, 84
Schrieber, Ira, 129
Schultz, Steve, 58, 78, 82
Schenkel, Charlie, 77
Schippert, John, 116, 118, 190, 196, 199-200, 202, 223
Schmidt, Del, 134, 143
Scott, Gary, 32
Scott, Gene, 164
Sears, Chuck, 151
Selenke, Jim, 118, 123
Selenke, Pius, 54, 118
Sewell, Howie, 182
Siefried, "Little Joe," 97, 201
Simmons, Phil, 152
Simon, Ken, 9
Shaddox, Chick, 92, 219, 222
Shane, Harvey, 44
Sheffield, James, 183
Shepard, Garland, 200
Sherrell, Len, 13
Shipley, John, 98
Shouse, Danny, 182-183
Shouse, Paul, 183
Shuck, Gordie, 7, 8, 11
Sikes, Jeff, 85, 100
Sinner, Lyle, 140
Skinner, James, 177, 221
Soderberg, Jerry, 192
Sorrells, Walter, 20
Snyder, Larry, 76
Smith, Bill (Speedway Motors), 10, 58, 66, 125-126, 133-134, 138-139, 141, 220, 223
Smith, Billy Joe, 109
Smith, Don, 146, 151, 162-163
Smith, Ed, 128, 136, 138, 140-141, 220
Smith, Hank, 38, 69, 78
Smyser, Sonny, 77
Snedeger, Red, 17
Snowden, Lonnie, 116, 120, 123, 183, 212-213,

Snyder, Larry, 76, 133, 135
Spain, Leon, 41
Sparks, Harold, 116-117, 194, 220
Sparks, Paul, 34
Speier, Don, 185, 223
Springer, Jim, 142
Stadeskev, Ron, 147
Stafford & Franklin, 176
Stanton, Gary, 211
Steinert, Les, 117, 172, 191, 194, 223
Stelzer, Dick, 11
Stephens, Lloyd K., 104, 213, 215, 222
Stepps, Charlie, 26, 48
Stewart, Jim, 146, 148, 223
Still, Rich, 10
Still, Roy, 10, 44, 46-47, 50, 219
Still, Roy & Hanna, Gary, 220
Stodola, Milo, 146
Stolfus, Ken, 75
Street, Freddie, 176
Stromer, Larry, 12
Strong, Bob, 152, 155, 223
Stone, Gary, 160
Stone, Jerry, 102, 111-112, 117, 119, 191, 208, 213, 215, 222
Stone, M. C., 111-112
Stoneking, Duane "Stoney," 82
Suchy, Pat, 106, 113, 167, 171, 173, 175, 177, 179, 201, 203, 207, 218, 221-222
Suggs, D. E., 92-93, 165, 186, 192, 201-202, 205-206
Suggs, Johnny, 204
Suhr, Jerry, 156, 222
Sundquist, Roger, 159
Sutcliffe, Dick, 23, 38, 49, 53, 55-56. 58-59, 71, 74-75, 78, 140, 142, 219-220
Swanson, Larry, 54, 83, 133-135, 139, 142, 220, 223
Swartz, Audie, 64
Swenson, Gary, 59, 140
Swindell, Sammy, 217

Sylvester, Dean, 62, 65, 217, 220

Taft, Junior, 85, 92-93, 96-98, 100, 102, 206, 222
Taylor, Benny, 11, 94, 171, 175, 203, 221
Taylor, Buddy, 71
Taylor, Ken, 15, 20, 27, 71
ter Steege, Dutch, 192-193
Teter, Brad, 61
Thomas, Eldon, 134
Thomas, Mike, 83
Thompson, Roger, 116, 118, 196, 202
Torrance, Del, 87, 90-92, 168, 169, 187, 199
Torson, Larry, 182, 213
Trade Winds Special, 123, 197, 208, 223
Trostle, Bob, 11, 70, 142, 217
Tullis, Fred, 91
Turner, Les, 61
Turpin, Charlie, 111

Uehling, Terry, 123, 195, 197, 208, 212, 223
Underwood, Bill, 23, 219
Ungar, Steve, 81
Upton, Larry, 130, 134, 220
Utz, Bill, 69, 72, 220

Valasek, Ray, 10
Van Beber, Jim, 85
Van Patten, Dave, 58, 76, 140, 142, 220
Van Sickle, Jim, 132
Vandervoort, Wes, 134
Vaughn, Les, 136
Vincent, Warren, 11
Vobach, Duane, 22, 44
Vonderfecht, Don, 163

Wade, Grady, 11, 108-109, 115, 199-200
Wagner, Earl, 62, 64, 66, 71, 74, 82, 220
Wagner, Frank, 79
Walinder, Mark, 212
Walker, Bobby, 174-175, 177, 180, 182, 221
Walker, Jack & Riffle, Kenny, 110
Walker, Jack, 175, 180

Walkingstick, Jerry, 212
Wallis, Bud, 16
Walter, Joe, 16
Walther, Ed, 147
Walton, Evert, 176, 204, 221
Ward, Bobby, 35
Ward, Dean, 10, 151, 156, 158, 221-222
Ward, Les & Beryl, 10
Waters, Curt, 138
Watson, Ed, 11
Watson, Rick, 11
Weber, Ray, 148
Weiland, Al, 47, 84, 86, 219, 221
Weld, Greg, 21-22, 25, 67-68, 220
Weld, Jerry, 15-17, 19, 21, 25, 27, 41, 51, 219
Weld, Kenny, 25, 69-71
Weld, Taylor "Pappy," 14, 21, 28-30, 35, 70-71, 74, 81
Wellendorf, Monty, 11
Wells, Charlie, 88
Weyhrich, Don, 159-161, 163, 222
Weyhrich, Lyle, 160-161
White, Bill, 40
Whitson, Jimmy, 165
Wickett, Jack, 106
Wilhelm, Warren "Jelly," 102, 107, 110, 116-117, 119, 131, 175, 198, 220
Wilkinson, John, 7, 220
Williams, Bob, 20-21, 28-29, 33, 35-37, 48-49, 56-57, 71, 74, 76, 81, 219-220
Williams, Charlie & Swenson, Gary, 59, 71, 74, 128, 133, 135, 219-220
Williams, Don & Foley, Richard, 27
Williams, Ken, 25, 41, 50, 56, 75, 219
Williams, Ron, 11, 150, 157, 159, 221-222
Williams, Ron & Ellett, Jim, 159, 221
Willingham, Kyle, 11
Willingham, Randy, 11, 206-207, 210
Wilson, Bob, 9
Wilson, Chet, 109, 118, 120
Wilson, Don, 158
Wilson, Jerry, 118, 120, 122, 176, 191, 197, 220

Wilson, Larry, 66
Winklebauer, Dick, 157
Wise, Jerry, 206-207
Wisley, Wayne, 98
Wittaker, Lyle, 43
Wolfe, Ervin, 85
Wolfe, Jackie, 85
Woolley, Gordon, 21, 45, 51, 65
Wood, Danny, 183
Woodside, Jay, 11, 24, 30, 35-36, 38, 59, 70-71, 78, 102, 110, 117-118, 174, 198-199, 203
Woodside, Pat, 11
Wright, Wayne, 51
Wyatt, Bud, 47, 49
Wyatt, Carl, 177, 221

York, Pete, 87

Zelmer, Dee, 197
Zink, Jack, 86-88, 91-93, 96, 97, 100, 103, 169, 199, 201, 204, 206-207, 215, 219, 221-222

Magazines and Periodicals

Hawkeye Racing News
Hot Rod
Kansas City Star
Lincoln Journal & Star
National Speed Sport News
Open Wheel
Racing Cars
Stock Car Racing
Topeka Capitol-Journal
Wichita Beacon

Yearbooks

Central Nebraska Racing Association Yearbook 1970, 1972-73
NCRA Yearbook(s) 1972-81 by Jack Ward
Nebraska Modified Racing Association 1964 Annual by Tony Wilson

Bibliography

Books

Decades of Daring by Bill Hill
Dialed In by John Sawyer
Dirt Track Legends, Vol. II by Lee O"Brien
The Dusty Heros by John Sawyer
The History of America's Speedways by Allan Brown
One Tough Circuit by Bill Hill
Racing's Real McCoy by Jack McCoy and Keith Sellers with Richard "Sterling" Hagerty
Roaring Roadsters by Don Radbruch
Roaring Roadsters #2 by Don Radbruch
Stand on the Gas by Joe Scalzo

HOME TRACKS

MIDWEST
27th & Superior
Lincoln, Nebraska

EAGLE RACEWAYS
Eagle, Nebraska

NEBRASKA MODIFIED RACING ASSOCIATION

1964 ANNUAL

PRICE $2.25

1975 NCRA YEARBOOK

PRICE $2.50

231